# The Buzz About
# *Boomer Brand Winners & Losers*

Warm, witty and thoroughly engaging, Barry Silverstein's thumbs up/thumbs down take on the brands, entertainment and events of their youth will make Boomers smile – maybe bug them too, if personal favorites rate as "losers." And marketers will enjoy this powerful primer on hidden histories that still influence Boomer consumer decisions today.

-    Barry Robertson, Partner, Boomer / neXt – consultants on brand regeneration in the 50+ space

If you're a Baby Boomer, *Boomer Brand Winners & Losers* will surely bring back cherished memories. This captivating book takes a comprehensive and engaging look at brands that impacted our lives, encouraging animated and fun debates about which are the best and worst of our generation.

-    Julie A. Gorges, author and blogger at *Baby Boomer Bliss*

*Boomer Brand Winners & Losers* brings one back to a simpler time with fond memories of favorite snacks and famous slogans. Barry Silverstein shares 156 winners and losers carefully selected and detailed. Enjoy the journey as you revisit forgotten brands from days gone by.

-    Dave Bernard, author, *I Want to Retire!* and blogger at *Retirement – Only the Beginning*

*Boomer Brand Winners & Losers* is a fun read, chock full of fascinating stories behind iconic brands. You may quibble with Barry Silverstein's designation of winners and losers, but you'll enjoy the humor, quirks and facts behind so many Boomer historic moments and brands.

- Toby Haberkorn, author, *Best Job Search Tips for Age 60-Plus*

What a fun trip down memory lane! Like song lyrics, some of these brands' marketing taglines are indelibly etched in my brain—and this book triggers a flood of feel-good associations. When talk turns to medical matters at your next Baby Boomer gathering (as it is wont to do, it seems, as we get older!), just pull out this book to get the conversation going in a more lighthearted direction!

- Roxanne Jones, co-author of the forthcoming book *Voices from the Other Side... of Retirement*

Anyone born before 1964 won't be able to read just one page of this book. For everyone born after 1964, you'll have 156 history lessons to learn from.

- David Wogahn, president, AuthorImprints and Boomer publisher

# Boomer Brand Winners & Losers

## 156 Best & Worst Brands of the 50s and 60s

Barry Silverstein

GW

GuideWords Publishing

GuideWords Publishing
5 Blue Damsel Court
Biltmore Lake, NC 28715 USA
www.guidewordspub.com

Cover Design by Charala
Book Layout © 2017 BookDesignTemplates.com

Boomer Brand Winners & Losers – Barry Silverstein -- 1st ed.
Library of Congress Control Number: 2019909733
Paperbound ISBN 978-0-9965760-6-2
Ebook edition ISBN 978-0-9965760-7-9

Printed in the United States of America

# Contents

Introduction: Still Relevant After All These Years .......................... 7

Television ................................................................................ 13

Cereal .................................................................................... 39

Soft Drinks ............................................................................ 53

Snack Foods ........................................................................... 67

Convenience Foods ................................................................ 81

Toys, Games and Comic Books ............................................. 95

Health, Beauty and Cigarettes ............................................ 109

Automobiles .......................................................................... 123

Fast Food .............................................................................. 137

Rock 'n' Roll ........................................................................ 151

Revolution ............................................................................ 165

Environment ........................................................................ 179

Technology ........................................................................... 193

Movies .................................................................................. 207

The Ultimate Boomer Brand Winner & Loser .................... 225

Appendix .............................................................................. 233

About the Author ................................................................ 267

# Still Relevant
# After All These Years

*I think I'm goin' back*
*To the things I learned so well in my youth...*
(Gerry Goffin and Carole King, "Goin' Back")

If you were born in the Boomer era (between 1946 and 1964), you grew up with all of the brands in this book. What is most remarkable about these brands is that many of them still exist today. This is no small feat: to be sustainable for more than fifty years, a brand has to evolve as times change and stay relevant to consumers.

The Boomer era was a time when the modern brand came to be, when brands reflected popular culture, and when brand advertising flourished. By the mid-60s, nearly half the population of the United States was under the age of 25, so advertising agencies aggressively targeted the Baby Boomer generation. The Boomer era was also a time when the medium of television revolutionized the way brands were marketed.

Two important ideas set the stage for this book:

1. My definition of "brand" is quite broad. Typically, a brand is a product with a brand name. I think of a brand as not just a product, but any person, place or thing that is widely known and evokes strong emotions. In addition to traditional products, I consider television shows, movies, songs, events and personalities to be brands because of the significant emotional impact they had on the Baby Boomer generation.

2. Everything during the Boomer era, and every Boomer-era brand, was influenced to some extent by television. This magic box brought the world into our living rooms, first in black-and-white and then, amazingly, in color. Television permanently changed media consumption in our country in the 50s and 60s, and it also became the primary gateway for brand advertising. Not surprisingly, brand advertisers used television to directly appeal to children, engage young minds and turn kids into product conduits to influence their parents. Television shows that directly appealed to Boomer kids were, in effect, brands. When we evaluate "Boomer Brands," they almost always are inter-connected with television. That's why the first chapter covers television shows in detail.

There are 156 brands in this book spanning fifteen chapters. The chapters represent brand categories. In deference to younger Boomers, and in recognition of important categories such as "Rock 'n' Roll" and "Revolution," some brands stretch beyond the 60s into the 1970s.

Within each category is a collection of brands that I designate as "Winners" and "Losers" – in my opinion, the best and worst brands of the Boomer era.

As a retired marketing professional, I viewed all of the brands in this book in the context of marketing, but I'm the first to admit there is likely to be a lot of personal bias in my "Winner" and "Loser" designations. I fully expect some readers to debate my choices, perhaps even heatedly. That would be a good thing, because it means they're as passionate about brands as I am. Still, I apologize in advance for any winner you think is undeserving and any loser you think got short shrift.

In defining "Winner" and "Loser," I applied the following broad criteria:

**Winner**

To be designated a "Winner" (look for the "thumbs up"), a brand must be iconic. It has to be authentic and relevant for the time. It has to have great appeal to Boomer kids as they were growing up. It has to have staying power and lasting influence. It has to be a brand that Boomers remember fondly to this day.

**Loser**

To be designated a "Loser" (look for the "thumbs down"), a brand has to be a strategic misfire, a marketing blunder, ahead of or behind its time, a short-lived fad, or a one-hit wonder. It has to be a brand that Boomers may remember – but if they do, it's probably with a good deal of derision.

For those readers new to this topic, *Boomer Brand Winners & Losers* is essentially a sequel to my first book, *BOOMER BRANDS: Iconic Brands that Shaped Our Childhood*. Fans of the first book thanked me for bringing back cherished memories about their favorite childhood brands. Some readers said the book inspired them to have spirited conversations about brands with spouses, siblings, friends, and even co-workers. Others let me know in no uncertain terms that I left out some Boomer-era brands that were meaningful to them. This book is far more comprehensive, including three times as many brands as in the first book. All of the material is new, so if you didn't read *BOOMER BRANDS* and you enjoy this book, check out the Appendix for a list of the brands included in the first book.

### How to Get the Most Out of *Boomer Brand Winners & Losers*

Each chapter of this book provides a brief discussion of a brand category, followed by what I hope are engaging stories about "Winners" (thumbs up) and "Losers" (thumbs down). Winners and losers appear one after the other to better high-light the differences. Each Winner and Loser occupies just a single page to make for optimum readability.

The final chapter identifies my selections for the Boomer era's "Ultimate Winner," one stellar brand that achieved lasting greatness, and "Ultimate Loser," one sorry brand that reached the pinnacle of success and then faded away into oblivion.

The Appendix contains a number of fun extras. Here you'll find links to old TV commercials that relate to the brands in this book, a handy form you can use to fill in your own choices for Boomer Brands you consider "Winners" or "Losers", and a discussion guide with suggestions for how to use this book in conversations.

You can read this book from start to finish, or you can read chapters or even individual brand stories in any order, based on your particular interests. Chapters are self-contained and the content has been organized to make it easy to browse, move around freely, stop anywhere, and reminisce.

Trademarks are valuable intellectual property, so they are always listed at the end of each chapter.

One of the things I truly appreciate about my fellow Baby Boomers is their thirst for knowledge. If you have an interest in expanded information beyond what you find in the pages of this book, I have included the sources I used for every brand covered.

If you would like free access to a special webpage that includes all of the source links from this book in one convenient reference, simply send your email address to:

guidewordspub@gmail.com

In the subject line, type: **WL Links**. You'll get a page link via return email. Your email will remain private and will not be shared or sold.

TV shows, movies, products and social movements of the 50s and 60s were a mirror of society when Boomers were growing up. Reminiscing about the brands of the Boomer era is good for the mind and the soul. It helps renew memories of a carefree childhood and happier times.

I hope "goin' back" to *Boomer Brand Winners & Losers* brings you lots of wonderful memories, encourages lively conversation, and perhaps even stimulates vigorous debate!

# Television

Whether you were born in 1946, 1964 or in between those years, you were part of the "view tube" generation. During our childhood, television first appeared in American homes. Like its predecessor, radio, television was free – with a very big string attached. That string, just like radio, was brand advertising.

Early on, television shows were interrupted by commercials, and many shows were sponsored by advertisers. It was not uncommon for a major advertiser's name to be a part of the show ("General Electric Theater," "Texaco Star Theatre"). In addition, the stars of some of these shows shamelessly shilled for products (for example, Dinah Shore famously crooned, "See the USA in Your Chevrolet").

Television was essentially divided into three time segments: Daytime, Primetime (evenings), and Weekends. Saturday mornings were reserved for children's programming; Saturday morning television shows included cartoons, filmed adventure series, and sometimes live presentations for children, and brand advertisers targeted Boomer kids directly.

Television shows themselves were really uniquely branded entertainment. Each show had its own timeslot, name, brand platform, distinct typeface, song, and branded characters or stars. The shows used brand merchandising to sell toys, games, and clothes. Television stars appeared in person at promotional events. Cereal, soft drink, snack food and other brands cleverly wove their products into the shows, a practice called "product placement" that started in the Boomer era and is now commonplace in TV shows and movies.

When it came to children's shows, Boomer kids had their own favorites. We sang along with the theme songs and pestered our parents to buy the brands we saw featured on the shows. Television programs aimed at Boomer kids were sometimes nothing more than vehicles for promoting various brands. Still, a Saturday morning television show was just as emotionally impactful to Boomer kids as the branded products the show advertised.

Daytime shows that appealed to Boomer kids were slotted in weekday mornings, largely aiming at youngsters ("Bozo the Clown," "Captain Kangaroo," "Ding Dong School," "Howdy Doody," "Romper Room"). In the afternoons, programming targeted adolescents and teens ("American Bandstand.")

Primetime featured entertaining television shows appropriate for the entire family to watch early in the evening, with more adult-oriented shows typically appearing after 9 PM. Family time in front of the television might have included popular Westerns, situation comedies, quiz shows, or variety shows. TV was truly a Boomer kid's window to the world.

## Adventures of Superman
### 1952 - 1958

"Adventures of Superman" was not just a winning television show, it featured a character who is undoubtedly one of the great American heroes of the 20th Century. Superman was first introduced in a 1938 comic book. He was then voiced on a radio show for eleven years before appearing in a feature film that led to the television series. Boomer kids thrilled to the Saturday morning adventure show, starring George Reeves as Superman, which began with those immortal words, "Faster than a speeding bullet! More powerful than a locomotive! Able to leap tall buildings at a single bound!" Filmed in black-and-white for the first two seasons, the show switched to color for the remaining six seasons. Little did we know that Superman's bright blue, yellow and red costume in color was really brown, gray and white for black-and-white filming! Kellogg's sponsored the show, and characters appeared in cereal commercials. Superman's immense popularity has continued to this day, through comic books, cartoons, movies, and merchandise.

Photo credit: Screen capture of George Reeves as Superman in the U.S. Treasury Department film, "Stamp Day for Superman," 1954, public domain

## The Pinky Lee Show
### 1954 - 1956

Pinky Lee was a burlesque comic who brought his brand of slapstick humor and zaniness to a children's television show. Filmed in front of a live studio audience of both parents and children, "The Pinky Lee Show" began with Pinky, dressed in a checkered jacket, singing and dancing frenetically, after which he would interact with audience members. This was followed by juvenile sketches, as well as what could loosely be termed a variety show, featuring comedians, singers, dancers, and performers, both humans and animals. What happened with the live audience was just as amusing as Lee's ad-libbed antics. Children sometimes asked inappropriate questions, while mothers participated in contests that were for the most part embarrassing. Lee unashamedly incorporated advertisers' products into the show. The most memorable moment came during a 1955 episode when Lee clutched his throat and passed out. Kids thought it was part of the show, but poor Pinky had taken ill on stage. The show lasted less than three years.

Photo credit: Photo of Betty Jane Howarth and Pinky Lee from the television show "The Pinky Lee Show," January 1954, public domain

## Adventures of Rin Tin Tin
### 1954 - 1959

Here's a winning combination: A boy and his dog (Rusty and Rin Tin Tin) paired with a Western. The story line featured Rusty, orphaned as the result of an Indian attack, improbably living at Ft. Apache as a "Corporal." Lt. "Rip" Masters was a kind of surrogate father to Rusty. Rin Tin Tin did all sorts of remarkable things, including fighting bad guys and generally maintaining law and order. The dog who played Rin Tin Tin was a descendant of the original "Rinty," a famous animal actor who starred in films of the 1930s and 1940s. At one point, he was the highest paid movie star in Hollywood. The television show appeared during a time when Westerns were wildly popular. The five seasons ran in the evenings, but the show was so endearing that reruns were shown on afternoons and Saturday mornings for decades afterwards, through at least the mid-1980s. In addition to the "Rin Tin Tin Club," the show spawned a wide array of merchandise including, of course, lunch boxes.

Photo credit: Photo of James Brown as "Rip" Masters and Rin Tin Tin from a postcard Brown sent to a fan of the television show, 1955, public domain

## Captain Gallant of the Foreign Legion
### 1955 - 1957

Appropriating the Western TV show formula, this program substituted an Arabian country for the Old West, a camel for a horse, and bad guy Arabs for Western bandits. Buster Crabbe starred in the show as Captain Gallant, who was the guardian of a young orphan boy, played by Crabbe's real son. (Hmmm – sounds like "Rin Tin Tin," doesn't it?) Crabbe was a real life superhero of his time: He was an Olympic medalist swimmer and film star who had the distinction of being the only actor to have played Tarzan, Buck Rogers, and Flash Gordon in film serials. The Foreign Legion, a branch of the French army, was romanticized in films, and Legionnaires, as members were called, were popular heroes. Real Legionnaires appeared in the show, which was first filmed in Morocco and later moved to Europe. After its three-year run on NBC, the show was renamed "Foreign Legionnaire" and syndicated, but it never quite matched the exalted status of its Western brethren.

Photo credit: Photo of Buster Crabbe as Captain Gallant from the television show "Captain Gallant and the Foreign Legion," circa 1955-1957, public domain

## The Adventures of Ozzie and Harriet
### 1952 - 1966

"The Adventures of Ozzie and Harriet" pioneered the family situation comedy format and may well have been one of the first TV reality shows. Based on the lives of the real Nelson family, the show started out on radio, transitioned to a feature film, and morphed into a television program that became one of the longest running series in history. The mastermind behind the show's success was the seemingly mild-mannered Ozzie Nelson, who negotiated a ten-year contract and was the show's creative firepower. The exterior of the Los Angeles house on the show was the Nelsons' actual home, and many of the happenings were appropriated from the Nelsons' daily lives. In fact, even though the fictional story lines were written for television, viewers thought the show represented the family's real life. The show was also used to launch Ricky Nelson's music career, reinvigorating the series in the 1960s. Reruns continued to air for decades once the show ended after its fourteenth year.

Photo credit: Publicity photo of Ozzie and Harriet Nelson from the television show "The Adventures of Ozzie and Harriet," ABC Television, 1964, public domain

## My Favorite Martian

### 1963 - 1966

"My Favorite Martian" was an absurd show based on an absurd premise: An alien crash-lands on Earth and is invited into the home of Tim O'Hara, a newspaper reporter who happens to see the spaceship descending to Earth. O'Hara covers for the alien by claiming he is his "Uncle Martin." Obviously, any viewer had to suspend reality to accept an extraterrestrial being who looked and sounded remarkably like an earthly human. And why wouldn't a reporter use the momentous event to write the biggest story of his career? But never mind all that. The show exposes the antics of Uncle Martin, played tongue-in-cheek by Ray Walston. Martin can do all sorts of quirky things, including communicate with animals, read minds, levitate objects, build time travel machines and more. Of course, only Tim knows the martian's real identity. Despite lasting just three seasons, "My Favorite Martian" was spun off into a short-lived cartoon TV series, a comic book, and a feature film. It also influenced other sci-fi shows, such as "Bewitched" and "Mork and Mindy."

Photo credit: Photo of Ray Walston as Uncle Martin from the television show "My Favorite Martian," CBS Television, 1963, public domain

## Sea Hunt

### 1958 - 1961

In its first season on television, "Sea Hunt" rapidly rose to a top-rated show. Highly unusual for its day because of the real underwater footage, the show follows Mike Nelson, a former U.S. Navy frogman who takes underwater assignments of all kinds. Lloyd Bridges, who played Nelson, didn't know how to scuba dive when the series first started, but he became skilled enough by the fourth season to do his own underwater stunts. To distinguish Mike Nelson from his adversaries under the sea's surface, he wears a double hose regulator and a light wet-suit while the bad guys wear single hoses and dark wetsuits. Since it was not feasible to film underwater dialogue, Bridges does a voiceover explaining the underwater action – a creative solution. At the end of each show, Bridges speaks directly to the audience about diving and ocean pollution, lending an air of environmental responsibility to the show. "Sea Hunt" inspired millions to take up scuba diving, Dell launched a series of "Sea Hunt" comic books, and a revival series aired in 1987.

Photo credit: Publicity photo of Lloyd Bridges, Tom Korman Assoc., 1966, public domain

## Circus Boy
1958 - 1961

The "boy and his dog" shows that aired in the 50s (such as "Rin Tin Tin" and "Lassie") led to a twist on the theme in "Circus Boy" – a boy and his elephant. Corky is orphaned when his circus performing parents are killed in a trapeze accident. He is adopted by Joey the Clown and stays with the circus as a water boy to Bimbo the elephant. Corky's new extended family members are the performers and workers who run the circus, fulfilling that childhood fantasy of running away and joining the circus for kids who watched the program. Unfortunately, other than Corky's pet-like relationship with Bimbo, the show didn't have much to offer in the way of a plot or action, so it ran just two seasons. The show's lasting legacy, though, was through its star, Micky Braddock, aka Micky Dolenz. He resurfaced as one of The Monkees, a rock band whose four members achieved success in the 60s as stars of a popular television show of the same name. In an episode of "The Monkees," Dolenz even sings part of the theme song from "Circus Boy."

Photo credit: Photo of Micky Dolenz under the name Micky Braddock as Corky from the television show, "Circus Boy," 1958, public domain

## Lassie

### 1954 - 1973

"Lassie," one of the most famous of the aforementioned "boy and his dog" genre, is also one of the most enduring. This TV show, which followed the adventures of a female collie and her companion, ran almost twenty seasons and won two Emmy awards early on. The show had as its inspiration seven feature films made between 1943 and 1951. The Lassie character remained throughout the series; she was played by six different male dogs provided by Rudd Weatherwax, a professional trainer who owned the original Lassie, also a male. Lassie outlasted both the show's venues and its cast members, which changed over the years. Some Boomers would have known Lassie's pal as Jeff (actor Tommy Rettig), while others would recall Timmy (actor Jon Provost). During the first decade, Lassie lived on a farm with either Jeff or Timmy, but the venue was later changed, somewhat strangely, to the U. S. Forest Service in an effort to broaden the show's appeal. Remarkably, "Lassie" was sponsored by Campbell's Soup for its entire run.

Photo credit: Photo portrait of Lassie from the television show "Lassie," 1956, public domain

## Mr. Ed
### 1961 - 1966

From boys and dogs, to men and... talking horses? "Mr. Ed" the horse first talked in a series of short stories written for children and published in 1937. But it was probably the 50s films about "Francis the Talking Mule" that prompted this TV sitcom to be created. Remember how Uncle Martin of "My Favorite Martian" fame would only reveal his alien powers to his friend Tim? Well, Mr. Ed, a horse who could inexplicably talk, only did so when he was with Wilbur, the human star of the show, played by Alan Young. There were gags galore related to Mr. Ed's verbalizing various clever lines and demonstrating that he was considerably more intelligent than Wilbur, who was somewhat of a sap. The most intriguing part of the series was the talking horse himself, played by a palomino named Bamboo Harvester. His voice was by an actor named Allan Lane, but the horse was so well trained that he reportedly really learned to move his lips!

Photo credit: Photo of the main cast of the television show "Mister Ed." Coulter-Strauss Public Relations for D'Arcy Advertising. D'Arcy was the ad agency for the program's sponsor, Studebaker. Circa 1961-1963, public domain

## The Flintstones
### 1960 - 1966

"The Flintstones," an animated television series by Hanna-Barbera, was the first to appear in prime time and remained the most successful animated network program until "The Simpsons" came along. Fred and Wilma Flintstone lived next door to Barney and Betty Rubble in a Stone Age world that comically represented a suburban America of the 60s. The show cleverly depicted such modern conveniences as cars, as if they existed in prehistoric times – only they were clunky wood and rock boxes propelled by running people. The show mimicked family situation comedies, most notably "The Honeymooners;" in fact, the Fred Flintstone character was based on Jackie Gleason's Ralph Kramden character. "The Flintstones" achieved remarkable popularity despite tepid critical reaction. The show aired for six seasons and reruns have been shown continuously since then. Subsequent TV shows, feature films, stage productions, comic books, and even theme parks have immortalized "The Flintstones."

Photo credit: Fred and Wilma Flintstone figurines at the Ankara Public Amusement Park, Nevit Dilmen, 2007, CC BY-SA 3.0

## The Jetsons
### 1962 - 1963

"The Jetsons" was Hanna-Barbera's futuristic counterpoint to "The Flintstones." But unlike the lengthy success of "The Flintstones," this animated television series lasted just one season. "The Jetsons" was a knock-off of "The Flintstones," set in the future instead of the Stone Age. It had similar characters, similar situations, and mirrored a family sitcom as did "The Flintstones." My thumbs down rating is based on its unoriginality in that regard, as well as its lack of longevity, even though new episodes were produced from 1985 to 1987 as part of another television show. Still, "The Jetsons" did depict the future in an innovative way. That's why the Smithsonian, for one, strongly disagrees with my negative assessment. In a 2012 series of articles that celebrated its 50th anniversary, Matt Novak wrote that the show "stands as the single most important piece of 20th century futurism" and it "has had a profound effect on the way that Americans think and talk about the future." By that standard, maybe "The Jetsons" isn't a loser after all!

Photo credit: The Jetsons cartoon card game, Mark Anderson, 2008, CC BY 2.0

## Bonanza
### 1959 - 1973

"Bonanza" was one of the two longest running Westerns on television, second only to "Gunsmoke." Ben Cartwright was depicted as a strong patriarch in a male-only household set on the fictional Ponderosa ranch near Virginia City, Nevada. Actor Lorne Greene, a Canadian, played Cartwright with finesse, amidst the distinct personalities of his three sons, Adam, Hoss and Little Joe. Producer David Dortort actually saw the family as a Western take on King Arthur (Cartwright) and his knights (his sons). Rather than ply the familiar Western plot lines of good guys and bad guys, "Bonanza" delved into family, relationships, and life on the ranch. Drama was interspersed with comedy, and social issues were bravely addressed. The show's influence was far-reaching. Television movies were produced, comic books and novels were published, merchandise was offered for sale, and reruns air to this day. The show also inspired the "Bonanza" and "Ponderosa" steakhouse chains.

Photo credit: Photo of the cast of the television show "Bonanza," from top: Lorne Greene, Dan Blocker, Michael Landon, Pernell Roberts, 1962, public domain

## The Big Valley
### 1965 - 1969

"The Big Valley" was so obviously a knock-off of "Bonanza" that I could not help but give it a thumbs down. Western? Check. Large ranch? Check. Family drama? Check. Four kids? Check. A strong parental figure? Check – except here, it's matriarch Victoria Barkley, played by Barbara Stanwyck. The show featured an almost ridiculous number of guest stars, including singer Lou Rawls, who made his acting debut as a black cowboy. Stanwyck won an Emmy for best dramatic actress in the show's first season, but "The Big Valley" was never a ratings hit. While "Bonanza" sustained its success well into the 70s, "The Big Valley" was cancelled after four seasons. Still, there are those who credit the show with pioneering an uncommonly strong female character for the Western genre. Two spin-off television series failed, only six issues of a companion comic book were published, and a feature movie based on the show, scheduled for 2012, was cancelled.

Photo credit: Photo of the cast of the television show "The Big Valley," from left: Richard Long, Linda Evans, Barbara Stanwyck, Peter Breck, and Lee Majors by wagon wheel, circa 1965, public domain

## Candid Camera
### 1948 - 1954, 1960 - 1967

Boomer kids and their parents alike loved the hilarity of America's first comedy reality show, "Candid Camera." Conceived by Allen Funt, a university research assistant, and first named "Candid Microphone," the show's premise was an immediate sensation: Catch people's authentic reactions to a variety of hoaxes with a hidden camera. The show debuted in 1948 and ran until 1954. For a period, it was incorporated as a feature of other shows, but it once again became a standalone program in 1960. The show's unique nature sometimes created problems with censors and sponsors but that didn't stop it from becoming one of television's most popular programs during its heyday from 1960 – 1967. Subsequent versions, including anniversary specials, have been produced in the U.S. and internationally since then, and the show was briefly revived for one season in 2014. "Candid Camera" is widely regarded as the forerunner of such successful reality shows as "America's Funniest Home Videos."

Photo credit: Photo of Allen Funt of the television show "Candid Camera," appearing on "The Dick Cavett Show," 1972, public domain

## Twenty-One
### 1956 - 1958

"Twenty-One" was a television game show that ultimately became symbolic of a major scandal. The game show pitted one contestant against another in an attempt to win 21 points for answering questions correctly. The concept seemed legitimate until then champion, Herbert Stempel, was defeated by a young, handsome college professor, Charles Van Doren. Van Doren's defeat of Stempel was of national interest; Van Doren even appeared on the cover of *TIME* magazine. It was later revealed, first by Stempel and then by another show contestant, that "Twenty-One" was fixed so that Van Doren would beat Stempel and win the game. After an investigation by the New York District Attorney's office confirmed the scam, the show was abruptly cancelled. Van Doren was nowhere to be found, but he eventually agreed to appear before a Congressional hearing in 1959, admitting to his participation in the fraud. Other game shows were also found to be fixed, but the genre survived. TV game shows are popular today, despite the early scandal.

Photo credit: Photo of Jack Barry and Charles Van Doren on the television show "Twenty-One," *TV Radio Mirror*, 1957, public domain

### The Ed Sullivan Show
#### 1948 - 1971

A Sunday night family tradition for most Boomer kids was watching "The Ed Sullivan Show." America's greatest variety show was hosted by a folksy, stiff and at times inept former newspaper columnist, but his real talent was knowing what people wanted to watch on television. In addition to airing a wide, eclectic variety of acts, the program was responsible for turning comedians and music performers into national icons. The range of entertainment was breathtaking, featuring everything from classical music (Itzhak Perlman appeared at age 13) to opera to Broadway musicals to circus acts. Younger Boomer kids loved the antics of Sullivan's puppet sidekick, "Topo Gigio," but as we got older, we thrilled to live appearances by countless rock 'n' roll performers, including Elvis Presley, The Supremes, The Rolling Stones, and perhaps most famously, The Beatles, who were virtually drowned out by screaming fans. In 1964, the live show averaged fourteen million viewers a week. "The Ed Sullivan Show" ran for an unprecedented twenty-three years.

Photo credit: Photo of Ed Sullivan and Fabian from the television show "The Ed Sullivan Show," CBS Television, 1959, public domain

## The Sonny and Cher Comedy Hour
### 1971 - 1974, 1976 - 1977

Sonny and Cher leveraged their musical success into a variety show that appeared on CBS television in 1971, ending because of their divorce in 1974. Originally intended as a summer replacement, the show was popular enough to attain a regularly scheduled time slot. The show consisted of banter between the two performers, comedy sketches, musical numbers, and guest appearances. At the end of each show, the couple sang their smash hit, "I Got You Babe." The program also gave Cher the opportunity to flaunt her extravagant costumes, which became part of her persona when she embarked on a solo career. Interestingly, when Sonny and Cher separated, they each managed to get their own individual television shows, if briefly. Then, in 1976, they reunited not in marriage but on television, in "The Sonny and Cher Show." Clearly, their previous magic fizzled, and so did the show after a short run. Cher went on to have a very successful musical career, while Sonny transitioned to politics, becoming a mayor and U.S. Congressman.

Photo credit: Photo of Sonny and Cher performing on "The Sonny and Cher Show," CBS Television, 1976, public domain

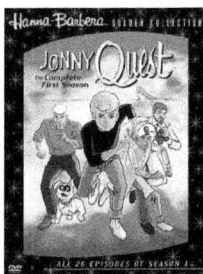

## Jonny Quest
### 1964 - 1965

"Jonny Quest" was an animated television show by Hanna-Barbera that started out in prime time. Despite lasting just one year, the show was so popular that reruns continued for twenty years, mostly on Saturday mornings. The series marked a new direction for Hanna-Barbera, known for such cartoon-like animations as "The Flintstones." Created by the comic book artist Doug Wildey, "Jonny Quest" was a more realistic, action animated series with a scientific slant. The main character, an eleven-year-old boy, accompanies his father, a famous scientist, on extraordinary adventures. "Jonny Quest" had outsized influence beyond its short prime time run. Merchandise related to the show included coloring books, coloring sets, comic books, a card game, a board game, puzzle sets, and a record. "The New Adventures of Jonny Quest" in the 1980s and "The Real Adventures of Jonny Quest" in the 1990s revived interest. Reportedly, there is a good chance a feature film is in Jonny's future. Thumbs up to an animated action series that won't die.

Photo credit: Cover of the DVD Hanna-Barbera Golden Collection, "Jonny Quest, The Complete First Season," copyright Warner Bros., released 2004

## The Dudley Do-Right Show
### 1969 - 1970

"The Rocky and Bullwinkle Show," an animated television series derived from two previous shows featuring the characters Rocky the flying squirrel and Bullwinkle the moose, was the creation of Jay Ward Productions. The Rocky and Bullwinkle franchise was so successful in the late 50s and early 60s that spin-off shows based on some of the other lovable characters seemed liked a logical next step. One of those characters, Dudley Do-Right, was a happy-go-lucky Canadian Mountie who got his own show. He was always doing battle with his archrival, Snidley Whiplash, over Do-Right's heart throb, Nell Fenwick. That story line goes only so far; Dudley was just fine in a minor character role, but promoting him to star of his own show turned out to be a dud. The animated series, which incorporated stories about Dudley with separate segments featuring other characters, lasted only one season, although it was later syndicated under a different name. Still, Dudley did inspire a live action feature film in 1999.

Photo credit: 'Happy Canada Day, Eh?' after Alex Anderson, Mike Licht, Flickr.com, CC BY 2.0

## Sources

*If you would like free access to a special webpage that includes all of the source links from this book, simply send your email address to: guidewordspub@gmail.com. In the subject line, type: WL Links. Your email will remain private and will not be shared or sold.*

*Television*
http://www.skooldays.com/blog/saturday-in-the-50s/
http://www.skooldays.com/blog/saturday-in-the-60s/

*Superman*
https://en.wikipedia.org/wiki/Adventures_of_Superman_(TV_series)
http://www.skooldays.com/categories/saturday/sa1414.htm
https://www.metv.com/lists/14-fascinating-facts-about-adventures-of-superman

*Pinky Lee*
https://en.wikipedia.org/wiki/Pinky_Lee
http://www.skooldays.com/categories/saturday/sa1353.htm

*Rin Tin Tin*
http://www.tv.com/shows/the-adventures-of-rin-tin-tin/
https://en.wikipedia.org/wiki/The_Adventures_of_Rin_Tin_Tin

*Captain Gallant*
http://www.skooldays.com/categories/saturday/sa1399.htm
https://en.wikipedia.org/wiki/Captain_Gallant_of_the_Foreign_Legion
https://en.wikipedia.org/wiki/French_Foreign_Legion

*Ozzie and Harriet*
https://en.wikipedia.org/wiki/The_Adventures_of_Ozzie_and_Harriet
https://www.littlethings.com/ozzie-and-harriet-facts/

*My Favorite Martian*
https://en.wikipedia.org/wiki/My_Favorite_Martian
https://io9.gizmodo.com/my-favorite-martian-is-a-seriously-weird-tv-show-and-y-1748783899

*Sea Hunt*
https://en.wikipedia.org/wiki/Sea_Hunt
https://fiftiesweb.com/tv/sea-hunt/
https://dtmag.com/thelibrary/sea-hunt-must-sea-tv/

*Circus Boy*
http://www.crazyabouttv.com/circusboy.html
https://nostalgiacentral.com/television/tv-by-decade/tv-shows-1950s/circus-boy/
https://en.wikipedia.org/wiki/Circus_Boy

*Lassie*
https://tvtropes.org/pmwiki/pmwiki.php/Series/Lassie
https://en.wikipedia.org/wiki/Lassie_(1954_TV_series)

*Mr. Ed*
https://en.wikipedia.org/wiki/Mister_Ed

*The Flintstones*
https://en.wikipedia.org/wiki/The_Flintstones
http://mentalfloss.com/article/81462/15-solid-facts-about-flintstones

*The Jetsons*
https://en.wikipedia.org/wiki/The_Jetsons
https://www.smithsonianmag.com/history/50-years-of-the-jetsons-why-the-show-still-matters-43459669/

*Bonanza*
https://en.wikipedia.org/wiki/Bonanza
https://www.neatorama.com/2011/06/23/17-facts-you-might-not-know-about-bonanza/

*The Big Valley*
https://en.wikipedia.org/wiki/The_Big_Valley
https://www.metv.com/lists/11-things-you-never-knew-about-the-big-valley-tvs-greatest-western-with-a-female-lead

*Candid Camera*
https://en.wikipedia.org/wiki/Candid_Camera
https://interviews.televisionacademy.com/shows/candid-camera

*Twenty-One*
https://en.wikipedia.org/wiki/Twenty-One_(game_show)
https://allthatsinteresting.com/charles-van-doren

*Ed Sullivan*
https://en.wikipedia.org/wiki/The_Ed_Sullivan_Show

https://interviews.televisionacademy.com/news/the-ed-sullivan-show-at-70-a-look-back

*Sonny and Cher*
https://en.wikipedia.org/wiki/The_Sonny_%26_Cher_Comedy_Hour

*Jonny Quest*
https://en.wikipedia.org/wiki/Jonny_Quest_(TV_series)
http://cartoonresearch.com/index.php/in-his-own-words-doug-wildey-on-jonny-quest/
https://www.forbes.com/sites/markhughes/2016/07/28/exclusive-jonny-quest-could-be-warners-next-big-franchise/#50eb7306749b

*Dudley Do-Right*
https://en.wikipedia.org/wiki/Dudley_Do-Right
https://en.wikipedia.org/wiki/The_Adventures_of_Rocky_and_Bullwinkle_and_Friends
https://nostalgiacentral.com/television/tv-by-decade/tv-shows-1960s/dudley-right-show/

The following trademarks and registered trademarks are the property of their respective holders: ABC, Adventures of Superman, The Adventures of Ozzie and Harriet, The Adventures of Rin Tin Tin, American Bandstand, The Big Valley, Bonanza, Bozo the Clown, Candid Camera, Captain Gallant of the Foreign Legion, Captain Kangaroo, Captain Midnight, CBS, Circus Boy, Chevrolet, Ding Dong School, Dell, Dudley Do-Right, The Ed Sullivan Show, The Flintstones, Francis the Talking Mule, General Electric Theater, Gunsmoke, Hanna-Barbera, The Honeymooners, Jay Ward Productions, The Jetsons, Jonny Quest, Kellogg's, Lassie, The Monkees, Mr. Ed, My Favorite Martian, NBC, The Pinky Lee Show, The Rocky and Bullwinkle Show, Romper Room, Sea Hunt, The Sony and Cher Comedy Hour, Texaco Star Theatre, TIME, Twenty-One

# Cereal

If there is one food inextricably linked to the Baby Boomer childhood, it is cereal. Boomers literally grew up with cereal. The cereal we all remember most was that crunchy, sweet stuff in colorful boxes. It's hard to believe that cereal manufacturers were able to take a cheap vegetable like corn, along with such grains as rice, wheat and oats, and turn that into virtually endless varieties of cereals we would crave. Of course, the "secret ingredient" wasn't any of those things – it was sugar.

The other secret ingredient wasn't edible at all – it was branding. General Mills, Kellogg's, Nabisco, Post, Quaker Oats, and other cereal companies were so adept at brand variation and extension that the cereal aisle became a dazzling display of colorful, creative packages concocted in the 50s and 60s.

Cereal existed prior to the Baby Boomer generation, but TV didn't. Television was a game changer. For the first time, cereal makers could not only advertise on this new medium, they could actually reach a new impressionable audience – children. By sponsoring children's and family television programs, cereal manufacturers and their brands immediately gained visibility with kids. But they did more than that: Cereal brands began to appear *within* programs, endorsed by television personalities who promoted those products during the shows and in accompanying commercials.

When it came to product packaging, cereal manufacturers quickly recognized that their boxes would be even more desirable if they featured characters that appealed to kids. Tie-ins between cereals and popular children's television shows were common. Cartoon characters like "Tony the Tiger" on boxes of Kellogg's Frosted Flakes were specially created to distinguish one cereal from another and grab the attention of children. The cereal boxes themselves acted as small billboards that called out to kids as their moms carted them around the grocery store.

Cereal manufacturers innovated in the use of cartoon mascots, prizes, games, cut-outs and contests. Some cereals offered toys and other merchandise in exchange for box tops; other cereals included small toys right in the box. Often, those cherished little items were related to a children's television show. Cereal companies were masters of brand extension – when a brand became popular, it wasn't long before flavor variations were spun off, or entire brand families were created.

While at least some modern cereals are notably "healthier," many of the sugary cereal brands that were beloved in the 50s and 60s remain on grocery store shelves today. And Boomers still love cereal – just like we did when we were growing up!

### Cap'n Crunch

In 1963, the Quaker Oats Company introduced a new cereal. Early television commercials for the cereal claimed, "It's got corn for crunch, oats for punch, and it stays crunchy, even in milk." In fact, Quaker employed a novel manufacturing technique, using oil to deliver crunch and taste, with a butterscotch flavor. No surprise that the name chosen was "Cap'n Crunch." Not only was it alliterative and descriptive of the cereal itself, the brand name also came to represent a cartoon character named Cap'n Crunch. He was more sophisticated than other cereal mascots because he was the brainchild of Jay Ward Productions, the same studio that conceived of Bullwinkle, Rocky, and a host of other well-known cartoon personalities. Cap'n Crunch was cleverly created to star in animated TV commercials, and Daws Butler, the voice of Huckleberry Hound and Yogi Bear, was chosen for the voice of Cap'n Crunch. Kids clamored for Cap'n Crunch right after its introduction. It soared in popularity. The brand family, at present with more than twenty-five variations, continues to expand. Cap'n Crunch was, and still is, a big winner.

Photo credit: A box of Cap'n Crunch, Famartin, Flickr.com, CC BY-SA 4.0

## Quake

In 1965, Quaker Oats tried something different: The company brought two new cereal brands to market at the same time. "Quake" and "Quisp," (so named to tie them in with "Quaker") each had a mascot, not surprisingly created by Jay Ward Productions, inventor of the "Cap'n Crunch" character. The "Quake" character was a miner and the "Quisp" character was an alien. The somewhat imposing miner was later transformed into a cowboy. Both cereals tasted pretty much the same but had different shapes. The really unique thing about these cereal brands, however, was the way Quaker Oats marketed them. They were almost always promoted together, and the alien (who was also named Quisp) would sometimes poke fun at the Quake brand. Obviously, this was intentional, because in 1972, Quaker Oats asked consumers to vote for the brand they liked best – either Quake or Quisp. The winner was Quisp, and Quake was discontinued the following year. Quaker Oats tried bringing Quake back a few years later under a different name, "Quangaroos," but once again it was pitted against Quisp and lost. Gone are the Quake and Quangaroos brands, but Quisp still exists.

Photo credit: Quake and Quisp "Kite Tail" comic book, davidd, Flickr.com, CC BY 2.0

### Cocoa Puffs and Cocoa Krispies

Both General Mills and Kellogg's, two behemoths who have been at war since the early days of cereal, created cocoa-flavored cereals in 1958. "Cocoa Puffs" by General Mills is a chocolatey version of "Kix" cereal. Its cartoon mascot, Sonny the Cuckoo Bird, famously proclaimed in commercials, "I'm coo-coo for Cocoa Puffs." While Sonny's physical appearance has changed over the years, he still finds his way onto boxes of Cocoa Puffs, which continue to be marketed. "Cocoa Krispies" by Kellogg's is a chocolatey version of "Rice Krispies," the venerable 1927 cereal that has since become a brand family with flavor varieties as well as "Rice Krispies Treats" and "Rice Krispies Treats Snap Crackle Poppers." If the latter sounds familiar, it's because "Snap, Crackle and Pop" are the little elves who have been on "Rice Krispies" cereal boxes since 1941. Cocoa Krispies, also still available today, has had a variety of cartoon mascots since its introduction; interestingly, those three elves have returned on modern-day boxes. Cocoa and cereal – a winning combination!

Photo credit: Cocoa Puffs, retro packaging, Theimpulsebuy, Flickr.com, CC BY-SA 2.0; Cocoa Krispies, Theimpulsebuy, Flickr.com, CC BY-SA 2.0

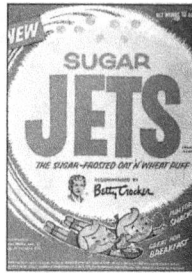

## Sugar Jets

In the annals of sugary cereals, there is a graveyard for brands that didn't make it for one reason or another. Introduced in 1953 by General Mills, "Sugar Jets" started life as "Sugar Smiles" and had a whole range of cartoon character endorsers, including the flying "Sugar Jets Kids," pictured on the early cereal box shown above, as well as the "Go-Cart Kids" and "Jet the Space Pilot." Somehow the cereal even managed to gain the recommendation of Betty Crocker. (In case you were wondering, "Betty Crocker" was not a real person, but a fictional character created to appeal to moms looking to buy baked goods.) Despite the support of all of these characters, though, the cereal never stayed in orbit. General Mills changed its name to simply "Jets" in an attempt to de-emphasize the large amount of sugar it contained. In addition, the cereal shape, originally similar to "Kix," was changed to look like space age elements, such as rockets and planets. Jets remained on the market until at least the late 60s but then crashed and disappeared.

Photo credit: A box of Sugar Jets, Breakfast Tarot, Flickr.com, CC BY 2.0

### Froot Loops

Kellogg's introduced "Froot Loops," a fruit-flavored cereal, in 1963. This was before freeze-dried fruit was being added to cereals, so absent any fruit, Froot Loops had a blended fruit flavor applied to its round red, orange and yellow "Loops." Kellogg's claimed each differently colored Loop was a unique flavor, but this scandalous untruth was exposed years later. Still, Fruit Loops was a popular cereal right from the beginning. One of the reasons could have been its cute cartoon mascot, "Toucan Sam," who continues to grace Froot Loops boxes. The rings on Sam's beak correspond to the original three colors, but additional colors have been added to modern-day Froot Loops. In television commercials, Sam would say, "Follow my nose! It always knows! The flavor of fruit! Wherever it grows!" in a voice that was created by the inimitable Mel Blanc, who also voiced Bugs Bunny, Daffy Duck, and Porky Pig. In addition to the original Froot Loops, Kellogg's has expanded the family to include "Fruit Loops Birthday Cake," "Wild Berry Froot Loops" and "Froot Loops Marshmallows," so the brand is still thriving.

Photo credit: A box of Froot Loops, Mike Mozart, TheToyChannel, Flickr.com, CC BY 2.0

## Kellogg's OKs

With the introduction of "Cheerios" in 1945, first under the name "CheeriOats" in 1941, General Mills had a winning cereal shape (round O's) and ingredient (oats). That wasn't "ok" with Kellogg's, so in 1959, "OKs" were introduced. They had a similar oat taste to Cheerios, but along with little "O's," this cereal contained little "K's." The first character to appear on the box was "Big Otis," a rather brawny-looking Scotsman dressed in traditional Scottish garb. Also appearing on the box was the slogan, "BR-R-AWNY NEW OAT CEREAL." It didn't take long before Kellogg's dropped the Scottish look for something more kid-friendly, namely, Yogi Bear. Yogi Bear was a cartoon character who first appeared on Hanna-Barbera's animated "The Huckleberry Hound Show" but was so popular he began to star in his own show in 1961. Since Kellogg sponsored the show, Yogi Bear was a natural tie-in for OKs. Yogi Bear appeared in television commercials for Kellogg's OKs, but to no avail – the cereal lasted just three years. Happily, Kellogg found another use for the equipment that manufactured OKs: It was re-purposed to make Froot Loops cereal!

Photo credit: Kellogg's OK cereal box front flat, copyright 1963, Kellogg's

### Lucky Charms

General Mills had a really good thing going with their Cheerios brand of cereal. As luck would have it, in 1964, the company started experimenting by adding bits of old-fashioned "circus peanuts" marshmallow candy to sugar-coated Cheerios. That's how "Lucky Charms," the first cereal with marshmallow bits, was born. Those "marbits," based on a charm bracelet, became the basis for a cereal that had the luck of the Irish behind it – as well as a cartoon mascot named "Lucky the Leprechaun." Lucky has changed in appearance over the years but the character has remained. The charms have been a differentiating feature for more than five decades. Included in the original formulation were green clovers, pink hearts, orange stars, and yellow moons. But General Mills got charm-happy as time progressed, adding blue diamonds, purple horseshoes, red balloons, green trees, pots of gold and later, more sophisticated charms, such as multi-colored rainbows and swirled color charms. There have even been limited edition charms. The astounding success of Lucky Charms has clearly been due to more than luck alone.

Photo credit: A modern-day box of Lucky Charms (front and back) with 1964 retro packaging, Mike Mozart, TheToyChannel, Flickr.com, CC BY 2.0

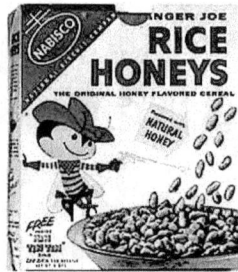

## Nabisco Rice Honeys

Looking to compete in the burgeoning Boomer cereal market, Nabisco purchased two different cereal brands and changed their names to "Rice Honeys" and "Wheat Honeys" in 1954. The two brands were often promoted together in television commercials featuring "Buffalo Bee," an anthropomorphized bee wearing a cowboy hat. The character didn't have the same sophistication as other cereal characters, and the cereals were nothing special either. Nabisco attempted to pump up cereal sales by adding little dinosaur prizes in the boxes and, later, with premiums that tied in with TV shows such as "Sky King" and movies such as "Mary Poppins" and the animated Beatles movie, "Yellow Submarine." The "Rice Honeys" name was changed to "Winnie the Pooh Great Honey Crunchers" in 1971 and a year later to "Klondike Pete's Crunchy Nuggets" in an effort to resuscitate a cereal that was losing its buzz. By 1975, the Klondike Pete's Crunchy Nuggets brand was no longer, and by then, Rice Honeys was merely a fading memory.

Photo credit: A box of Nabisco Rice Honeys, bigdogLHR, Flickr.com, CC BY 2.0

### Trix

"Silly rabbit! Trix are for kids!" If you don't remember that phrase from the 1959 Trix commercial, you may not have been paying attention, since it's still in use. So is "Tricks," the Trix Rabbit, who was inspired by a hand puppet and replaced an early mascot, a flamingo, as the Trix mascot. An updated rabbit appears on boxes today. General Mills created "Trix" by giving its "Kix" cereal a serious sugar boost and three fruit flavors: "Lemony Yellow," "Orangey Orange," and "Raspberry Red." Other flavors and colors have been added since. The cereal has always retained its spherical ball shape, except for a period of time in the 90s when fruit shapes appeared, only to be replaced by the balls again in 2007. Tricks the rabbit was such an icon that he became the subject of a contest run twice by General Mills, in which kids were asked to vote on whether or not Tricks should be allowed to eat a bowl of Trix. (Poor Tricks never had the pleasure.) Children voted overwhelmingly "Yes!," so Tricks the rabbit is seen enjoying a bowl of Trix in later commercials.

Photo credit: A box of Trix, Mike Mozart, TheToyChannel, Flickr.com, CC BY 2.0

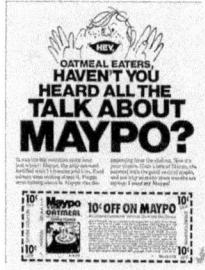

## Maypo

In 1953, more than ten years before Quaker Oats made instant oatmeal an integral part of the breakfast cereal mix, a small Vermont company, Maltex, introduced "Maypo," the world's first maple flavored oatmeal cereal. Three years later, Marky, an animated boy wearing a cowboy hat, proclaimed "I want my Maypo!" in a television commercial. Marky connected with Boomer kids, catapulting the hot cereal to instant fame. A series of Maypo commercials that followed starred such high-profile sports personalities as Mickey Mantle and Johnny Unitas shouting the same catchy phrase. In the mid-60s, along came Quaker Oats with its own brand of instant oatmeal, followed in the 70s by an ever-increasing number of flavored oatmeal varieties, including, of course, maple flavor. That sent sales of the Maypo brand plummeting. The cereal was eventually sold to another company. These days, you can purchase "Maypo Instant Maple Oatmeal," but it isn't really representative of the original product. Marky lives on, however; he still appears on the box!

Photo credit: 1976 magazine ad for Maypo cereal, Flickr.com, public domain

## Sources

*If you would like free access to a special webpage that includes all of the source links from this book, simply send your email address to: guidewordspub@gmail.com. In the subject line, type: WL Links. Your email will remain private and will not be shared or sold.*

*Cap'n Crunch*
https://en.wikipedia.org/wiki/Cap%27n_Crunch
https://www.mrbreakfast.com/cereal_detail.asp?id=53

*Quake*
https://www.mrbreakfast.com/cereal_detail.asp?id=294
http://nightflight.com/quisp-vs-quake-the-breakfast-feud-between-cereals-from-outer-and-inner-space/

*Cocoa Puffs, Cocoa Krispies*
https://en.wikipedia.org/wiki/Cocoa_Puffs
https://www.mrbreakfast.com/cereal_detail.asp?id=82
https://en.wikipedia.org/wiki/Cocoa_Krispies
https://www.mrbreakfast.com/cereal_detail.asp?id=80

*Sugar Jets*
https://gunaxin.com/a-tribute-to-discontinued-cereals

*Froot Loops*
https://en.wikipedia.org/wiki/Froot_Loops
https://www.mrbreakfast.com/cereal_detail.asp?id=142

*Kellogg's OKs*
https://www.mrbreakfast.com/cereal_detail.asp?id=263
http://www.mikanet.com/museum/item.php?item=2210

*Lucky Charms*
https://en.wikipedia.org/wiki/Lucky_Charms
https://www.mrbreakfast.com/cereal_detail.asp?id=222
http://mentalfloss.com/article/55538/50-year-history-lucky-charms-65-marbits

*Rice Honeys*
https://www.mrbreakfast.com/cereal_detail.asp?id=312
https://leeduigon.com/tag/wheat-honeys-and-rice-honeys/

*Trix*
https://en.wikipedia.org/wiki/Trix_(cereal)
http://mentalfloss.com/article/74134/11-colorful-facts-you-might-not-know-about-trix-cereal

*Maypo*
https://en.wikipedia.org/wiki/Maypo
https://www.mrbreakfast.com/cereal_detail.asp?id=234

# Soft Drinks

During the Boomer era, soft drinks were the preferred beverage for most kids.

Whether you called it soda, soda pop, pop or tonic, the carbonated soft drink tickled our collective fancy because it was sugary sweet and bubbly. We craved the non-carbonated soft drink too: It was generally nothing more than flavored sugar water with fruit juice. Drink mixes, also popular when Boomers were growing up, rounded out the soft drink category.

Older Boomers were likely to be introduced to soda at a Woolworth's lunch counter, a drug store, a diner, or a drive-in. For the most part, sodas served up in the 40s and 50s came by the glass from a soda fountain. Syrup was mixed with carbonated water. More popular than a lonely glass of soda, though, was the ice cream soda. Remember root beer floats?

The other most likely place to come in contact with soda was the fast food establishment. Burger joints and other fast food restaurants were popping up in the 50s and 60s. Arch-rivals McDonald's and Burger King accelerated the "cola wars," each aligning with a competing cola company – McDonald's with Coca-Cola and Burger King with Pepsi-Cola.

Bottled soda was portable and readily available to kids. Who can forget those early, clunky refrigerated bins that held bottles of ice-cold goodness? Later, we bought our bottled soda from vending machines with the little attached metal bottle opener.

In 1957 the aluminum can was introduced, and in 1962, along came the pop-top. That made it even easier for us to buy, carry and open cans of the sweet stuff... no bottle opener needed.

Lots of Boomer kids were Coke or Pepsi (or maybe Royal Crown) cola fanatics, but there were plenty of other flavors to choose from: quirky Dr Pepper; A&W and Hires root beer; 7 Up, Sprite and Squirt citrus flavors; Nesbitt's Orange and Orange Crush orange soda, to name a few. The diet soda craze started during the Boomer childhood as well.

On the non-carbonated side, you may have had a hankering for Hawaiian Punch, Kool-Aid or Tang. Chances are you were a juice drinker, too – you probably preferred either Mott's Apple Juice or Welch's Grape Juice. And maybe you remember those chocolate drinks of yesteryear, Chocolate Soldier and Yoo-hoo.

All of these beverages had something in common – they were part of the American lifestyle. Boomer era advertising tended to reflect this in no uncertain terms: We'd see images of kids and their families at home, having picnics, on the beach, on a road trip – guzzling soft drinks like they were actually good for you. Soft drink marketers were relentless in making sure we saw their product ads, everywhere we turned. Soft drinks were an integral part of growing up in the 50s and 60s.

### Dr Pepper

Dr Pepper has the distinction of being the oldest major brand soft drink in America. It was invented by Charles Alderton, a pharmacist for Morrison's, a drug store in Waco, Texas, in 1885. That's one year *earlier* than the invention of Coca-Cola. From the very start, Dr Pepper was different: It had a unique name, the origin of which is still murky, and a unique flavor, which is concocted from twenty-three different ingredients. The soft drink was introduced at the 1904 World's Fair in St. Louis, which also saw the introduction of the ice cream cone. Dr Pepper pioneered the "pepper" flavor category of soft drinks. Not surprisingly, Dr Pepper has had a long, contentious relationship with Coca-Cola. Dr Pepper sued the Coca-Cola Company in 1951 and again in 1972. The second suit, regarding trademark infringement, forced Coca-Cola to change the name of a short-lived beverage. Later, two proposed Coca-Cola/Dr Pepper mergers fell through. Today, Dr Pepper is part of the Dr Pepper Snapple Group and it is still going strong. And as you may have noticed, there's no period after "Dr" in Dr Pepper!

Photo credit: Dr Pepper bottles, Mike Mozart, TheToyChannel, Flickr.com, CC BY 2.0

## Royal Crown Cola

Royal Crown Cola got its start in an early 1900s dispute over Coca-Cola syrup. Grocer Claude Hatcher of Columbus, Georgia was unhappy with the price, so he started a company called Union Bottling Works and created his own soft drink, which he named "Royal Crown." The first product was a ginger ale. After expanding into other flavors, the company's name changed first to Chero-Cola and later to Nehi. Chero-Cola was reformulated in 1934 and renamed "Royal Crown Cola." In its heyday, Royal Crown became known as an innovator. It was the first soft drink company to distribute its products in cans in 1954, and the first to come out with a low-calorie diet cola, "Diet Rite," in 1958. Royal Crown Cola seemed to hit its peak in the 50s, when it was being aggressively promoted. Despite its popularity back then, the cola has lagged behind Coca-Cola and Pepsi-Cola in recent years. Today, the flagship product is known as "RC Cola," and wouldn't you know it, the cola is now a product of the Dr Pepper Snapple Group.

Photo credit: Royal Crown Cola sign, Gerry Dincher, Flickr.com, CC BY-SA 2.0

## 7UP

7UP is widely regarded as the first nationally successful lemon-lime soda. Less widely known is that an original ingredient in the 1929 formulation was lithium citrate, a patent medicine product popularized in the late 1800s and early 1900s as a mood stabilizer. It was removed in 1948. Still, that led Charles Leiper Grigg, who created the soft drink, to give it the odd name "Bib-Label Lithiated Lemon-Lime Soda." Thankfully, it was changed to "7UP Lithiated Lemon-Lime Soda" and shortened to "7UP" by 1936. There are many theories surrounding the origin of the 7UP brand, but there is no definitive reason for the name. 7UP was different from the popular colas of the day because it was a clear color and contained no caffeine. Advertising for 7UP always attracted attention. In the 50s, the soft drink was described as "fresh" and used the slogan, "You like it... it likes you!" 7UP is probably best known, though, for its daring repositioning as the "UNCOLA" from 1969 to 1975, when Peter Max style psychedelic images and TV commercials with Geoffrey Holder set the drink apart from competitors. Today, the 7UP brand is owned by the Dr Pepper Snapple Group.

Photo credit: 7UP sign, Joanna Poe, Flickr.com, CC BY-SA 2.0

## Squirt

Lemon-lime worked for "7UP," and orange worked for "Crush," so why not a grapefruit soda? Herb Bishop created "Citrus Club" in 1938 and bottled it in Phoenix, Arizona. With further experimentation, Bishop formulated a grapefruit juice and sugar soft drink that, to him, tasted like a squirt of juice coming from a section of grapefruit, so he named the new soda "Squirt." To promote the soft drink, he and a partner created a cartoon mascot named "Little Squirt," who appeared in advertising in the 40s and 50s. Squirt had less sugar than many soft drinks at the time, so it achieved a certain popularity, sometimes more as a mixer than as a stand-alone soda. The real problem for Squirt: It was destined to become a niche player. The soft drink couldn't possibly compete with 7UP or a growing list of fruit-flavored soft drinks. What's more, Squirt never had the huge marketing budgets of competing soft drinks. Even so, Squirt could have easily sunk into oblivion, but it continues to be sold today, in original, Ruby Red, and Diet versions. Squirt is pitched as a "caffeine-free Thirst Quencher," and it, too, is owned by the Dr Pepper Snapple Group.

Photo credit: Squirt advertisement, 1950s Unlimited, Flickr.com, CC BY 2.0

## Sprite

The dominance of Coca-Cola in the soft drink industry is hard to deny, and Sprite is a living example of it. This citrus-flavored soft drink, referred to as "lymon," (a combination of "lime" and "lemon") is owned by Coca-Cola. The Sprite brand is currently number three in worldwide soda sales (and second only to Coke in Coca-Cola's product line). Sprite started out in 1959 as "Clear Lemon Fanta" in Germany. Coca-Cola owned Fanta and wanted a carbonated soft drink to compete with 7UP, so they brought the German product to the United States in 1961, renaming it "Sprite." Sprite was an immediate hit. The distinctive green "dimpled" bottle, augmented by its green packaging, reinforced Sprite's unique positioning. Sprite has remained fresh and vibrant, introducing an updated logo, new ad slogans, and numerous product variations, such as "Sprite Ice," "Sprite on Fire," and "Sprite Remix." In recent years, Sprite promotion has included tie-ins with LeBron James and major hip hop stars. Sprite is a superb example of a soft drink that stays relevant and continues to delight a growing audience.

Photo credit: Sprite case, Mike Mozart, TheToyCannel, Flickr.com, CC BY 2.0

## Nesbitt's

In 1924, the Nesbitt Fruit Products Company, founded by Hugh Nesbitt in California, created and sold syrups for soda fountains. In 1938, "Nesbitt's Orange" was launched as a bottled soda with 10 percent California orange juice. Other bottled flavors followed, but Nesbitt's Orange remained the flagship product. The challenge for Nesbitt's: "Orange Crush," first marketed in 1911, was the leader in orange soda market share. Orange Crush had pieces of orange pulp in the original formulation. Despite the fierce competition, Nesbitt's Orange did manage to become the top-selling orange soda brand in the late 1940s and 50s. A young actress named Marilyn Monroe appeared in a 1946 ad for Nesbitt's, and Nesbitt's sponsored a 50s children's television show, "Ricky and the Magic Trolley." In 1955, Nesbitt's Orange was selected as Disneyland's "Official Orange Drink." By the late 60s, however, Nesbitt's Orange had to compete not only with Orange Crush, but against Fanta, a Coca-Cola brand. That crushed Nesbitt's popularity and Nesbitt's was eventually sold. The brand has been resurrected in recent years and is now available in three flavors.

Photo credit: Nesbitt's sign, Joanna Poe, Flickr.com, CC BY-SA 2.0

## TaB

When consumers became more calorie-conscious in the sexy 60s, soft drink manufacturers took note. Royal Crown's Diet Rite may have been the first diet cola to be introduced in 1958, but rival Coca-Cola responded with the launch of TaB (small "a" to stand out) in 1963. The new product was actually the Coca-Cola Company's first entry into the diet cola market. Ads asked the question, "How can one calorie taste so good?" Apparently, the name "TaB" was derived from a computer-generated list of thousands of possibilities, and the word "tab" was tested with consumers. The story goes that prospective buyers liked it because they could "keep tab" on their weight. TaB had to change its formulation when one of its ingredients, cyclamate, was banned by the FDA in 1969, but that didn't affect the cola's considerable popularity. The 1970s saw flavor variations of TaB, and then a caffeine-free version came along in the 1980s. When Diet Coke was introduced in 1982, sales of TaB predictably declined, but the brand was not abandoned. Even though TaB has continued to be a cult favorite, rumors of the brand's impending demise persist to this day.

Photo credit: TAB ad, *The Globe and Mail*, Jamie, Flickr.com, CC BY 2.0

### Flav-R-Straws

Milk was a cereal additive, not the beverage of choice for Boomer kids. Our parents, though, were always trying to get us to drink more milk. Food manufacturers solved the problem, turning milk into a kind of soft drink by adding flavoring with syrups, such as Bosco and Hershey's Syrup, and powders, such as Nestle's Quik and Ovaltine. In 1956, along came a new, interactive way to enhance milk, "Flav-R-Straws." These strange little contraptions looked like paper straws and supposedly dispensed chocolate, strawberry, or coffee (really... coffee?!) flavor when kids sucked on them. The result was less than stellar – it took a lot of sucking, the taste was tepid, and the color the straws made the milk was sickening. Still, Flav-R-Straws managed to get the "Good Housekeeping Seal of Approval." The product was discontinued in 1961, largely because the straws were too expensive to compete with syrups. But it turns out Flav-R-Straws were simply ahead of their time. They inspired "Milk Magic" in the U.S. and "Sippahs" in Australia, both more modern, technologically advanced versions of Flav-R-Straws.

Photo credit: Flav-R-Straws, 1957 magazine ad, public domain

## Kool-Aid

Kool-Aid is a real American success story. It was invented by Edwin Perkins, a Midwesterner who began tinkering with liquid concoctions in his mother's kitchen at age twelve. Perkins started a family business to manufacture and sell household products. One product, "Fruit-Smack," was a concentrated liquid that turned water into six flavorful drinks. Inspired by Jell-O, a childhood favorite of his, Perkins experimented and figured out how to dehydrate Fruit-Smack. In 1927, he named his new product "Kool-Ade," but because of trademark issues changed it to "Kool-Aid" in 1934. Packaging the product was another challenge: Perkins had to develop a special inner liner to keep Kool-Aid fresh. Along the way, Perkins pioneered POP (Point Of Purchase) promotion, creating a counter carton that allowed six flavor packets to be displayed at once. He even offered cash bonuses to distributors of the product. Kool-Aid became an inexpensive Depression era drink and continued its meteoric rise from there. Today, the Kool-Aid line includes powders, liquids and juice packets.

Photo credit: Kool-Aid point of purchase display, Diane Webb, Pexels.com

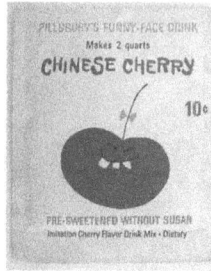

### Funny Face

Think of rivals Kraft and Pillsbury as the Coca-Cola and Pepsi-Cola of the convenience food market. Kraft acquired the Kool-Aid brand and arch-rival Pillsbury wanted to eat into the powdered drink's market share. An ad agency came up with "funny faces" to represent each flavor of a drink powder, and the "Funny Face" brand was born in 1964. Not a bad idea – until two of the flavors were named "Injun Orange" and "Chinese Cherry." The "Injun" package sported a cross-eyed cartoon character with war paint and feathers, while a face with slants for eyes and buck teeth was featured on the "Chinese" package. Complaints poured into Pillsbury. Less than a year later, the company changed the offending names to "Jolly Olly Orange" and "Choo Choo Cherry," in keeping with the original flavors, "Goofy Grape," "Rootin' Tootin' Raspberry," and "Freckle-Face Strawberry," (apparently not insulting, since strawberries kind of have freckles). Other flavors followed, as did premiums such as mugs and pitchers. The drink mixes lasted until 1994, but the brand never quite shook its early packaging controversy.

Photo credit: Funny Face packet, bigdogLHR, Flickr.com, CC BY 2.0

## Sources

*If you would like free access to a special webpage that includes all of the source links from this book, simply send your email address to: guidewordspub@gmail.com. In the subject line, type: WL Links. Your email will remain private and will not be shared or sold.*

*Dr Pepper*
https://drpeppermuseum.com/history/
https://en.wikipedia.org/wiki/Dr_Pepper

*Royal Crown Cola*
https://www.drpeppersnapplegroup.com/brands/rc-cola
https://en.wikipedia.org/wiki/RC_Cola

*7UP*
https://en.wikipedia.org/wiki/7_Up
https://www.metv.com/stories/a-history-of-7up-told-through-14-fascinating-ads
https://dangerousminds.net/comments/the_uncola_7up_and_the_most_psychedelic_lsd-friendly_ad_campaign_of_all_tim

*Squirt*
https://blog.retroplanet.com/soda-pop-of-the-week-squirt-soda/
https://www.squirtsoda.com/

*Sprite*
https://www.coca-colacompany.com/stories/primary-color-why-sprite-has-sported-green-since-1961
https://www.rewindandcapture.com/why-is-sprite-called-sprite/
https://www.cokesolutions.com/products/articles/sixty-years-of-sprite.html

*Nesbitt's*
https://www.nesbittsorange.com/facts.htm
https://en.wikipedia.org/wiki/Nesbitt%27s
https://en.wikipedia.org/wiki/Crush_(soft_drink)

*TaB*
https://en.wikipedia.org/wiki/Tab_(drink)
https://www.snopes.com/fact-check/keeping-tab/

*Flav-R-Straws*
https://en.wikipedia.org/wiki/Flav-R-Straws

https://www.newsfromme.com/2015/01/15/flav-r-straws/

*Kool-Aid*
http://kool-aiddays.com/history/
https://en.wikipedia.org/wiki/Kool-Aid

*Funny Face*
https://food52.com/blog/18562-maybe-these-pillsbury-drink-mix-mascots-are-best-left-in-1965
https://en.wikipedia.org/wiki/Funny_Face_(drink_mix)

The following trademarks and registered trademarks are the property of their respective holders: 7Up, A&W, Bosco, Burger King, Chero-Cola, Chocolate Soldier, Coca-Cola, Coke, Crush, Diet Coke, Diet Rite, Disneyland, Dr Pepper, Fanta, Flav-R-Straws, Funny Face, Good Housekeeping, Hawaiian Punch, Hershey, Hires, Jell-O, Kool-Aid, Kraft, Lymon, McDonald's, Milk Magic, Mott, Nehi, Nesbitt's, Nestle, Orange Crush, Ovaltine, Pepsi, Pepsi-Cola, Pillsbury, Quik, RC Cola, Royal Crown, Sippahs, Snapple, Sprite, Squirt, TaB, Tang, Uncola, Welch, Woolworth, Yoo-hoo

# CHAPTER 4

# Snack Foods

Boomer kids may have considered snack food essential fuel, but the 1960 edition of the Merriam-Webster Dictionary classified it as "junk food." This broad categorization could include candy, cookies, chewing gum, potato chips, ice cream and much more. The pejorative "junk food" also applied to fast food, which we'll get to later.

Historically, Boomers were far from the first American generation to get hooked on snacks. The Hershey chocolate bar was invented in 1900. At the St. Louis World's Fair in 1904, cotton candy and waffle cones with ice cream were thrilling 20th Century children. The Oreo cookie was introduced in 1912, Life Savers in 1913, and Tastykakes in 1914. Even the Girl Scouts began selling cookies in 1917.

The Roaring Twenties may have been the Jazz Era, but it was also the era of modern candy, with such product introductions as Baby Ruth, Butterfinger, Milky Way, Oh Henry! and Reese's Peanut Butter Cups. In the 1930s, along came Fritos, Lay's, Snickers, Tootsie Pops and Twinkies, arguably the ultimate

Boomer junk food. The 1940s spawned such memorable snacks as Almond Joy, Jolly Ranchers, Junior Mints, M&Ms, Whoppers, and Cheetos.

So why are snack foods so closely associated with kids of the 50s and 60s? Not surprisingly, television had a lot to do with it. Television was an ideal promotional vehicle for snack foods. Like cereal, snack foods found their way into children's television programs. The so-called "boob tube" was also a natural when it came to snacking. What could be better than vegging out in front of the TV while scarfing down chips, popcorn, bite-sized candies, or any other salty or sweet snack?

Snack foods were promoted in myriad other ways during the Boomer era – magazines, newspapers, comic books, radio, billboards and that most potent of all promotions – in grocery, drug and candy stores.

Interestingly, the post-World War II manufacturing boom also contributed to snack foods, not just in terms of food production, but in novel and convenient packaging. This was a time when bags, boxes, tins and other bright, bold food containers were ingeniously designed to have kid appeal.

It was a serious challenge to limit "winners" and "losers" in the snack food category to a relative handful. There are so many classics that Boomer kids craved, I could write an entire book devoted just to Boomer era snack foods. Hmmm. Now *there's* a sweet idea...

## Barnum's Animal Crackers

Animal crackers first appeared in England in the 1800s. They were produced in the U.S. by the Stauffer Biscuit Company in 1871, but the best-known brand, Nabisco "Barnum's Animals," launched in 1902. Why does this ancient crunchy cookie rate as a Boomer era winner? Because most every Boomer kid probably snacked on animal crackers in pre-adolescence. But there have been some big changes to animal crackers since their early days. The original box, as you may recall, was designed with a string handle so it could be hung on a Christmas tree. The illustrated animals were always shown in cages, much like in a circus train boxcar. In 2018, however, the animals were "set free," a year after the Ringling Brothers and Barnum & Bailey Circus closed down, so now the animals on the box are depicted cageless. The cookies started out as vaguely animal-shaped, but in the Boomer era (1958), a new production method was introduced. That's when rotary dies were used to include more intricate detail on each cookie. Scores of animals have been made into animal crackers by Nabisco. Munch some today!

Photo credit: Barnum's Animal Crackers, Willis Lam, Flickr.com, CC BY-SA 2.0

## Atomic Fireballs

Return with me to 1954, during the height of the Cold War... just nine years after two atomic bombs were dropped on Japan by the United States, and five years since the Soviet Union exploded the atomic bomb. Boomer kids were practicing "duck and cover" under their school desks. Some folks were building bomb shelters in their backyards. The entire nation had a morbid fascination with the utter destruction that could result from nuclear war. Along came "Atomic Fireballs" to radiate heat. It goes without saying that the name of this red-hot candy was in poor taste, but certainly in keeping with the preoccupation of the day. The taste was said to be cinnamon – but it was another secret ingredient that lit the fire in our young mouths: capsaicin, naturally found in such peppers as chili and jalapeno. The hardness was rock-like – so Atomic Fireballs were fondly called "jawbreakers." Boomer kids had contests to see how long they could keep this confection in their mouths. Some kids swore by them... I swore at them. Despite being a loser in my book, Atomic Fireballs bewitch kids to this day.

Photo credit: Vintage Atomic Fire Ball sign, public domain

## Cheetos

Can a snack food be responsible for a corporate merger? Yes, in the case of "Cheetos." The first puffed cheese snack was invented in 1948 by Fritos creator Charles Doolin. Cheetos were so popular that the Frito Company couldn't make them fast enough. To meet demand, Doolin partnered with potato chip producer Herman Lay. That led to the 1961 merger of their two companies, forming Frito-Lay Inc. First came Crunchy Cheetos; it wasn't until 1971 that Cheetos Puffs were introduced. The Cheetos production technique included a cheese hydration process that was pioneered by the U.S. military. Cheetos were engineered to melt so quickly in a human's mouth that we're tricked into thinking the body is not consuming calories. No wonder we couldn't eat just one (which later became the slogan for Lay's potato chips). An animated cartoon mouse appeared in 1971 TV commercials as the first Cheetos mascot, but "Chester Cheetah" is the Cheetos mascot today. The top-selling cheese snack is sold in a mind-boggling 50 flavors in over 20 countries worldwide, with some flavors unique to each country.

Photo credit: Cheetos bags, Mike Mozart, TheToyChannel, Flickr.com, CC BY 2.0

## E-Z Pop

Sometimes, the original product is a loser while a later competitor is a winner. This was famously the case with the ill-fated Hydrox cookie, which was introduced *before* look-alike Oreo, the highly successful sandwich cookie. The same thing happened to Benjamin Coleman's clever 1953 invention, the first self-contained popcorn popping pan – a predecessor to microwave popcorn, which wasn't commercially available until the 1980s. Coleman's unique product was marketed by the Taylor-Reed Corporation in 1954 under the brand name "E-Z Pop." Five years later, Frederick Mennen marketed "Jiffy Pop," an extremely similar product he claimed to invent. The Jiffy Pop brand was then sold to American Home Products. By the early 60s, Jiffy Pop ate into E-Z Pop's sales and Taylor-Reed sued. The company actually won the law suit, but it was overturned on appeal. The result spelled doom for the now defunct E-Z Pop brand. Jiffy Pop, today manufactured by Conagra, remains on the market, still using its original slogan: "As much fun to make as it is to eat."

Photo credit: E-Z Pop box from a 1954 ad, public domain

### Drake's

Drake's and Hostess were two bakeries that could each lay claim to the hearts (and stomachs) of Boomer kids. While Hostess was churning out Ho Hos, Ding Dongs, Sno Balls and Twinkies, Drake's was matching them, cake for cake, with Devil Dogs, Ring Dings, Yankee Doodles, and Yodels. Drake's was started by New York baker Newman Drake in 1896. Kids may have first come into contact with Drake's through the now famous "Devil Dog," introduced to the snack world in 1926 and continuing as a perennial favorite with generations of children, including Boomer kids. "Yankee Doddles" followed in 1928. Drake's really started pumping out the products we loved in the 50s and 60s; "Ring Dings," "Funny Bones," "Yodels," and "Fruit Doodles" (renamed "Fruit Pies") made their appearance back then. That cute little duck was on all the packaging. Strangely enough, Drake's was acquired by Interstate Bakeries, who also owned Hostess, in 1998. But in 2013, Drake's was again separated from its snack cake rival when it was purchased by McKee Foods. Sweet!

Photo credit: Drake's Devil Dog, Evan Amos, CC0 1.0, public domain

## Bonomo Turkish Taffy

It was a hard decision that I had to chew on: Was Bonomo Turkish Taffy a winner or a loser? True, the product has resurfaced today, in its original flavors, as a "retro candy." Still, Turkish Taffy is one of those candies that was bad for Boomer kids in two ways, both hard and soft: It had to be smacked and cracked into pieces yet it was pliable. Consumed hard or soft, Turkish Taffy wreaked havoc on young teeth, even if kids loved it. Invented in 1912 in New York by Herman Herer, it became known as "Bonomo Turkish Taffy" when the Bonomo family purchased taffy maker M. Schwarz & Sons in 1936. At first, Turkish Taffy was sold in large sheets at Woolworth stores, where sales clerks would break it into pieces with a hammer. In the 1940s, the candy was packaged into bars, first only in vanilla flavor. Chocolate, strawberry, and banana flavors came later. In 1949, Bonomo Turkish Taffy had the dubious distinction of originating "The Magic Clown," one of the very first children's television programs tied in so closely with the product sponsor that the clown himself was named Bonomo.

Photo credit: Bonomo Turkish Taffy, P F, Flickr.com, CC BY-SA 2.0

## M & M's

Mars and Hershey collaborated to produce "M & M's" in 1941. Chocolate was being rationed due to World War II. Forrest Mars Sr., son of Mars Company founder Frank Mars, teamed up with Bruce Murrie, son of William Murrie, president of Hershey Chocolate, to manufacturer M & M's (named after Mars & Murrie) using Hershey's chocolate. The unique hard shell, which prevented the chocolate from melting, was such a big hit with the U.S. Army that it was sold exclusively to the military until the war ended. When Boomer kids and their parents got hold of M & M's, they couldn't keep their hands off of them. The 1949 slogan said it all: "Melts in your mouth, not in your hand." A year later, the iconic lower-case "m" was imprinted on each morsel and has been there ever since. Plain M & M's were joined by Peanut M & M's in 1954. A slew of colors and flavors have followed in each decade. The animated characters representing the little candies have become stars in their own right. In the U.S. alone, over 400 million little M & M's are churned out by Mars each day. The candy is sold in over 100 countries.

Photo credit: Peanut butter M&Ms, Cathy Stanley-Erickson, Flickr.com, CC BY-ND 2.0

## Necco Wafers

Another one of those candies Boomer kids loved or hated was Necco Wafers. A puff of sugared powder always seemed to emerge when you unwrapped these hard little circles of questionable goodness. Most of the flavors were yucky... I think the licorice was the worst. Well, maybe the chocolate was okay. Necco Wafers did manage to have something of a cult following when Boomers were growing up. First produced in 1847, they got their name from the New England Confectionary Company (NECCO). As with M & M's, Necco Wafers were a hit with the military in World War II – they were virtually indestructible when shipped and didn't melt. Boomer kids became the next likely audience. The company attempted to change the recipe in 2009 but, after complaints, returned Necco Wafers to the original formulation. In 2018, NECCO filed for bankruptcy and production of Necco Wafers was halted. But wait! The candy brand has been purchased by Spangler Candy Company and is likely to be resurrected.

Photo credit: Necco Wafers, Mike Mozart, TheToyChannel, Flickr.com, CC BY 2.0

## Popsicle

The flavored ice pop Boomer kids came to know and love was created by accident. In 1905, 11-year old Frank Epperson left a cup of soda with a stirring stick in it on the porch. The soda froze overnight, and Frank found what looked like an icicle on a stick the next morning. It inspired him to offer his "Epsicle" to friends at school. Later, his own kids loved it, calling it "Pop's sicle." Frank loved the catchy name, so he patented the product in 1923 and began to sell his "frozen drink on a stick." Soon after Popsicles were made available, Frank's company was sued by Good Humor, an ice cream company that was already selling frozen ice cream treats on a stick from trucks. The Popsicle Corporation agreed to pay Good Humor a license fee so they could continue to make "frozen suckers" from flavored ice. What goes around comes around – but not for a while. It wasn't until 1989 that Good Humor bought the rights to Popsicle. All through the 50s and 60s fruit-flavored Popsicles delighted Boomer kids, who loved the sweet refreshing treats.

Photo credit: Popsicle bag, Joad Henry, Flickr.com, CC BY-ND 2.0

## Pixy Stix

This product was originally intended as a powdered drink mix called "Frutola," produced in the 1930s. The inventor, J. Fish Smith, saw that kids liked eating the stuff straight, so he changed the name from Frutola to "Fruzola" (no one is quite sure why) and sold it with a spoon. In 1952, the product was re-branded "Lik-m-Aid." It wasn't until 1959 that the colorful "Pixy Stix" sugar-filled straws came along – just in time for Boomer kids. Eating candy was one thing parents seemed to begrudgingly tolerate, but pouring sugar down our little throats brought snacking to a whole new insidious level. Pixy Stix also made one heck of a mess on hands, clothes, and floors. They became controversial and were roundly criticized by parents, along with other absurd, nutritionally bankrupt treats such as those candy necklaces and waxy bottles with colored sugar water in them. Regardless, Pixy Stix survived. They even went on to become a weird faux cocaine substance; snorting lines of Pixy Stix sugar actually gained popularity over the years. Today Pixy Stix are sold under the "Wonka" brand.

Photo credit: TheDeliciousLife on VisualHunt.com, CC BY

## Sources

*If you would like free access to a special webpage that includes all of the source links from this book, simply send your email address to: guidewordspub@gmail.com. In the subject line, type: WL Links. Your email will remain private and will not be shared or sold.*

*Snack Foods*
https://www.bonappetit.com/restaurants-travel/article/a-history-of-american-snack-foods-from-waffle-cones-to-doritos

*Barnum's Animals Crackers*
https://en.wikipedia.org/wiki/Animal_cracker
http://mentalfloss.com/article/78447/11-wild-facts-about-animal-crackers

*Atomic Fireballs*
https://en.wikipedia.org/wiki/Ferrara_Candy_Company#Atomic_Fireballs
https://brooklynbrainery.com/blog/what-makes-atomic-fireballs-candy-so-spicy
http://www.candyblog.net/blog/item/atomic_fireballs

*Cheetos*
https://en.wikipedia.org/wiki/Cheetos
https://www.thrillist.com/eat/nation/things-you-didnt-know-about-cheetos

*E-Z Pop*
https://midwestmaize.wordpress.com/2017/07/31/e-z-pop/
https://en.wikipedia.org/wiki/Jiffy_Pop
https://www.jiffypoppopcorn.com/

*Drake's*
https://en.wikipedia.org/wiki/Drake%27s_Cakes
https://drakescake.com/1/heritage

*Bonomo Turkish Taffy*
http://bonomoturkishtaffy.com/MuseumHistory ep 40.html
http://www.bonomoturkishtaffy.com
https://en.wikipedia.org/wiki/Turkish_Taffy

*M&M's*
https://en.wikipedia.org/wiki/M%26M%27s
http://www.mms.com/

*Necco Wafers*
https://en.wikipedia.org/wiki/Necco_Wafers
https://www.spanglercandy.com/our-brands/necco-wafers

*Popsicle*
https://en.wikipedia.org/wiki/Popsicle_(brand)
https://www.popsicle.com/our-story

*Pixy Stix*
https://www.candyfavorites.com/history-pixy-stix-candy
https://www.foodbeast.com/news/pixy-styx-facts/

The following trademarks and registered trademarks are the property of their respective holders: Almond Joy, Atomic Fireballs, Baby Ruth, Barnum's Animals, Barnum & Bailey, Bonomo Turkish Taffy, Butterfinger, Cheetos, Cheetos Puffs, Chester Cheetah, Conagra, Crunchy Cheetos, Devil Dogs, Ding Dongs, Drake's, E-Z Pop, Fritos, Fruit Doodles, Funny Bones, Girl Scouts, Good Humor, Hershey, Ho Hos, Hostess, Hydrox, Jiffy Pop, Jolly Ranchers, Junior Mints, Lay's, Life Savers, Lik-M-Aid, Mars, McKee Foods, Merriam-Webster, Milky Way, M&M's, Nabisco, Necco Wafers, Oh Henry!, Oreo, Peanut M & M's, Pixy Stix, Popsicle, Reese's Peanut Butter Cups, Ring Dings, Ringling Brothers, Snickers, Sno Balls, Spangler, Stauffer, Tastykake, Tootsie Pops, Turkish Taffy, Twinkies, Whoppers, Wonka, Yankee Doodles, Yodels

# Convenience Foods

Post-World War II American society was hungry for change. The economy was booming and technological innovation in manufacturing was flourishing. Those factors made the Boomer era ripe for "convenience foods."

At first, moms everywhere frowned upon products that came in cans, boxes, bottles and bags. They couldn't be taken seriously because the food wasn't fresh. Canned food had been rationed during the war. Frozen foods weren't widely available until refrigerators with freezers were sold to American families.

When the number of supermarkets in the country doubled between 1948 and 1958, and the electric kitchen became commonplace in homes, convenience foods gained traction. The idea of faster, easier food preparation started to take hold. It would skyrocket when microwave ovens became affordable in the mid 60s.

Clarence Birdseye began experimenting with quick frozen vegetables in the early 1900s, but his products found a willing market in the 50s. Swanson Foods used some of Birdseye's freezing techniques to create the first TV dinners in 1954. It wasn't long before competitors flocked to frozen foods. The canned goods and packaged foods categories exploded at the same time. Moms began relying on convenience foods to save time, doctoring them up so they would mimic meals prepared from scratch. Convenience foods became major time-savers for entertaining as well.

Convenience foods caught on with Boomer kids, too. For instance, we had the awesome individual power to concoct our very own peanut butter and jelly sandwiches – simply by scooping stuff out of two jars and smearing it on white bread. We could turn ordinary milk into a yummy sweet drink just by mixing in chocolate syrup or powder. And once freezers came along, we could have our very own stash of prepackaged ice cream available to us, day and night.

Television and magazine advertising helped fuel the popularity of convenience foods. Food companies published scores of cookbooks in the 50s with recipes that coached moms on how to use convenience foods to create complete meals and even gourmet dishes. Appearing in 1950, "Betty Crocker's Picture Cookbook" was the first of more than 250 Betty Crocker cookbooks that have been published since then.

At the time, little thought was given to sugar, salt, carbohydrates, fat, cholesterol, preservatives, or artificial flavors and colors in processed and packaged convenience foods. Health consciousness would emerge later. But one thing is certain: Convenience foods achieved mass adoption in the 50s and 60s, and Boomer kids were part of that food revolution.

## PB&J

"Peanut butter and jelly sandwich" is not a brand, but it may as well be. This iconic creation, which traces back to the early 1900s, was popular with World War II soldiers. It then became a Boomer era staple, thanks to convenience foods. Every Boomer kid knew PB&J well, because it was in so many of our lunch boxes: Take two pieces of white bread, slap on some peanut butter (creamy or crunchy, depending on your preference), and finish it off with a helping of jelly (most often grape, although other flavors were allowed). The brands behind this carb- and fat-laden combination were often Wonder bread, Skippy peanut butter, and Welch's grape jelly (although competitive brands may have been substituted). "Wonder Bread" was the first pre-sliced bread sold nationally in 1930, apparently inspiring the phrase, "the greatest thing since sliced bread." The "Skippy" brand of peanut butter was launched in 1932, four years after the introduction of "Peter Pan" peanut butter. Welch's grape jelly started out as "Grapelade" in 1918. Put them all together and presto! You have a Boomer kid's beloved meal.

Photo credit: Peanut butter and jelly sandwich, keri', Flickr.com, CC BY 2.0

## Smucker's Goober

For the peanut butter and jelly purist, "Smucker's Goober," first introduced in 1968, was pure heresy. It combined "stripes" of creamy peanut butter with grape or strawberry jelly. Doesn't this severely limit the distinct individuality of PB&J sandwiches by reducing our ability to smear more (or less) peanut butter, vs. more (or less) jelly on the bread? But for those of us who were simply too *lazy* to stick our knives in two separate jars, I suppose Smucker's Goober met a need. In fairness to Smucker's, the brand name was a powerhouse in the 60s. In 1962, the renowned advertising tag line was introduced: "With a name like Smucker's, it has to be good." Early on, Smucker's made ketchup and pickles, but the company was recognized primarily for its jellies and spreads. It also made peanut butter, produced separately and as an ingredient in Goober. Perhaps it is fitting that "goober" has become known to mean someone foolish... like a person who might not want to apply peanut butter and jelly separately!

Photo credit: Smuckers Strawberry Goober, Willis Lam, Flickr.com, CC BY-SA 2.0

## Catsup/Ketchup

Elsewhere in this book you'll see a reference to the "cola wars," during which Coca-Cola, Pepsi-Cola and other brands fought it out for soft drink superiority. Lesser known is the "ketchup war," which began during the Boomer era, when two leading brands, "Heinz Ketchup" and "Hunt's Catsup," competed in the condiment category. Back then, Americans loved their tomato catsup or ketchup (same product, different spelling). It was an accompaniment to hamburgers, meat loaf and the like. Boomer kids may have even tried to get away with ketchup sandwiches. Even today, somewhere around 97 percent of American homes have a bottle of ketchup handy. Frankly, the ketchup war was no contest in the 50s and it's still no contest today. Hunt's, with about 20 percent market share, has always played catch up to Heinz, with about 60 percent market share. Fact is, Heinz pioneered ketchup in 1876 before Hunt's was even founded in 1888. Similar to the Coca-Cola brand being the perennial cola leader, the Heinz brand has been and continues to be the ketchup leader. You might say it put Hunt's in a real pickle.

Photo credit: 1957 Hunt's Catsup ad, *Reader's Digest* magazine, SenseiAlan, Flickr.com, CC BY 2.0

## SPAM

I expect I'll get a number of "spam" emails for having the nerve to categorize "SPAM" as a loser. I must admit the SPAM brand story is impressive. Introduced by Hormel Foods in 1937, it was the only canned meat product at the time that didn't require refrigeration. As a result, SPAM was the perfect food for GIs during World War II. They even used the residue to grease their guns and waterproof their boots! After the war, American homes readily embraced the stuff, maybe because it was their patriotic duty to do so... or maybe they heard the "Hormel Girls" singing about it on the radio... or maybe the sugar, salt and fat content made it positively addictive. Whatever the reason, SPAM became a staple in the diet of many Boomer kids. By 1959, Hormel had sold one billion cans of SPAM; today over eight billion cans have been sold in 44 countries worldwide. Granted, SPAM is a celebrated brand, with its own museum, cooking festival, NASCAR car, and Broadway-inspired show ("Spamalot"). It's hard to argue with that kind of brand marketing success... but unhealthy SPAM is still a loser in my book.

Photo credit: SPAM can, Mike Mozart, TheToyChannel, Flickr.com, CC BY 2.0

### Log Cabin Syrup

If you ever had pancakes or waffles as a kid (and who didn't?), you probably ate them with "Log Cabin" syrup. The Log Cabin brand was extra special because it was originally packaged in its own little log cabin tin. Minnesota grocer Patrick Towle introduced the brand in 1887 in honor of Abraham Lincoln, who grew up in a log cabin. Maple syrup was already sold in cans, but it was Towle who patented the unique log cabin tin in 1897. After General Foods acquired the brand in 1927, food packaging was more sophisticated. Illustrated details were added and the log cabin became the colorful container that charmed Boomer kids in the 50s and 60s. In 1987, a limited edition of the Log Cabin tin was produced to celebrate the brand's 100th anniversary. As for the syrup inside, Towle was so proud of the quality of his maple syrup that he originally offered a $500 reward to anyone who could present evidence of adulteration. Towle produced a pure maple syrup product as well as one blended with cane sugar. Log Cabin is still sold today by Conagra.

Photo credit: 1962 Log Cabin ad, 1950sUnlimited on VisualHunt.com, CC BY

## Aunt Jemima

While the "Aunt Jemima" brand still exists, it is a sad symbol of our country's history with slavery and racism. Charles Rutt and Charles Underwood teamed up to market a pancake mix in 1889. Rutt had attended a minstrel show, popular at the time, and saw a performance set to a tune called "Old Aunt Jemima." It was about a slave mammy of the plantation South. The song inspired Rutt to brand the mix "Aunt Jemima." When Rutt and Underwood couldn't market it successfully, they sold the brand to Davis Milling Company in 1890. Davis hired Nancy Green, who was born a slave, to personify the Aunt Jemima character. Green traveled the country pitching the pancake mix and the product became a success. Subsequent Aunt Jemima characters made live appearances, and in the 30s and 40s, Aunt Jemima even had her own radio show. By the 50s, the Aunt Jemima character was firmly embedded in American culture. Other products, including syrup, were introduced under the brand name by Quaker Oats, who acquired the brand. Protests against the Aunt Jemima brand name have continued since the 60s.

Photo credit: Aunt Jemima syrup, Mike Mozart, TheToyChannel, Flickr.com, CC BY 2.0

## Kraft Singles

"PB&J" may be the #1 sandwich of choice for Boomer kids, but grilled cheese is probably a close second. The grilled cheese sandwich, American style, has been around since the 1920s, but World War II helped propel it to popularity when Navy cooks prepared them, usually with just one slice of bread and melted grated cheese on top. When "Kraft Singles" were introduced in 1949, grilled cheese sandwiches with cheese between two pieces of bread could be slapped together in no time. The individually wrapped slices were actually formed from a manufactured, processed "cheese food." Today's version of Kraft Singles is described as a "Pasteurized Prepared Cheese Product" because the Food and Drug Administration doesn't consider it "cheese," plain and simple. Be that as it may, this innovative little product single-handedly influenced the do-it-yourself version of the modern-day grilled cheese sandwich. Boomer kids also liked to eat it plain. It was great to play with too. While a wide variety of cheese is available today, it's estimated that Kraft Singles are found in almost half of American households.

Photo credit: Kraft Singles, Mike Mozart, TheToyChannel, Flickr.com, CC BY 2.0

## SpaghettiOs

Maybe your family had a weekly "spaghetti night" when you were a kid. So how did that beloved pasta dish wind up in a can as "SpaghettiOs"? You can thank Campbell Soup employee Donald Goerke, "the Daddy-O of SpaghettiOs." He created the O-shaped pasta for the Franco-American brand, owned by Campbell, so it wouldn't slip off a kid's fork or spoon. The product was introduced in 1965 with a television ad in which singer Jimmie Rogers crooned, "Uh-Oh, SpaghettiOs!" SpaghettiOs began sharing shelf space with other processed pasta products, such as Chef Boy-ar-dee "Beefaroni" (canned) and Kraft "Macaroni & Cheese" (boxed). Why do I classify the product as a loser? The original SpaghettiOs had an unremarkable bland taste, and it was positively slimy sliding down your throat. Plus, that starchy pasta swimming in a watery tomato base was notably bereft of nutritional value. Despite all this, some kids loved it. Some kids still do. SpaghettiOs are available today under the Campbell name. They come in numerous varieties, some cans labeled with comic book and video game characters.

Photo credit: SpaghettiOs, theimpulsebuy, Flickr.com, CC BY-SA 2.0

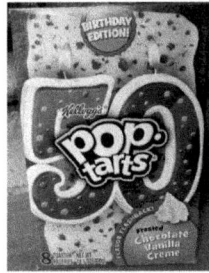

### Pop-Tarts

"Pop-Tarts" was arguably one of Kellogg's most successful inventions – and it was rushed to market to upend a competitor's product. Post had already announced a toaster pastry called "Country Squares," but just six months after its introduction in 1964, Kellogg debuted a similar product. Ironically, it was developed by one of their food technologists named Bill Post. Kellogg very cleverly piggy-backed onto the trendy success of Andy Warhol's "pop art" to create the name "Pop-Tarts" and a breakfast winner was born. Post scrambled, renaming their product "Toast-em Pop-ups" to no avail. A few years later, Nabisco introduced "Toastettes," but they couldn't compete either. The Pop-Tarts brand today remains the king of the toaster pastries. Pop-Tarts turned the common toaster, previously used only to toast bread, into an instant breakfast machine. Still, plenty of people (not just kids) eat them straight from the box. Nowadays, Pop-Tarts remain popular. They come in a kazillion flavor varieties, all containing loads of sugar.

Photo credit: Pop-Tarts 50th Birthday box, Mike Mozart, TheToyChannel, Flickr.com, CC BY 2.0

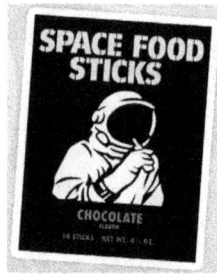

## Space Food Sticks

This questionable product was actually introduced in the early 1970s, technically after the Boomer era. But Pillsbury's "Space Food Sticks" are so indicative of food fad failures that they are deserving of the "loser" designation. Boomer kids were fascinated with space travel back then. Maybe they wondered how the heck astronauts ate food up there. Pillsbury worked with NASA to come up with a nutritional substance in the shape of a long stick that astronauts could feed through their helmets to feed themselves. Space travel had already created a market for "Tang," an orange powder made by General Foods that was used to flavor water for NASA astronauts – so Pillsbury followed the same marketing strategy with Space Food Sticks. Introducing them to consumers as "non-frozen balanced energy snack[s] in rod form" and packaging them in space age silver foil didn't make them more appealing. When interest in space flagged and the name was changed to "Food Sticks," the product fizzled. Still, food industry experts credit the ill-fated Space Food Stick with being the forerunner of today's energy bar.

Photo credit: Space Food Sticks label, public domain

## Sources

*If you would like free access to a special webpage that includes all of the source links from this book, simply send your email address to: guidewordspub@gmail.com. In the subject line, type: WL Links. Your email will remain private and will not be shared or sold.*

*Convenience Foods*
https://www.womenshistory.org/articles/how-highly-processed-foods-liberated-1950s-housewives
https://emilycontois.com/2014/04/28/archive-adventures-1-the-oh-so-glamorous-world-of-velveeta-cheez-whiz/
https://emilycontois.com/2012/10/04/curating-the-history-of-american-convenience-cuisine/
https://livinghistoryfarm.org/farminginthe50s/life_15.html

*Peanut Butter & Jelly*
https://www.nationalpeanutboard.org/news/who-invented-the-peanut-butter-and-jelly-sandwich.htm
https://en.wikipedia.org/wiki/Peanut_butter_and_jelly_sandwich
https://en.wikipedia.org/wiki/Wonder_Bread
https://en.wikipedia.org/wiki/Skippy_(peanut_butter)
https://en.wikipedia.org/wiki/Peter_Pan_(peanut_butter)

*Smucker's Goober*
http://mentalfloss.com/article/74156/10-things-you-might-not-know-about-smuckers
https://www.smuckers.com/products/peanut-butter

*Catsup/Ketchup*
https://www.nationalgeographic.com/people-and-culture/food/the-plate/2014/04/21/how-was-ketchup-invented/
https://en.wikipedia.org/wiki/Ketchup
https://en.wikipedia.org/wiki/Heinz_Tomato_Ketchup
https://en.wikipedia.org/wiki/Hunt%27s

*SPAM*
https://www.smithsonianmag.com/food/how-spam-went-canned-necessity-american-icon-180963916/
https://en.wikipedia.org/wiki/Spam_(food)
https://www.spam.com/about

*Log Cabin syrup*
http://maplesyruphistory.com/category/log-cabin/
https://en.wikipedia.org/wiki/Log_Cabin_syrup
https://www.logcabinsyrups.com/

*Aunt Jemima*
https://blackexcellence.com/aunt-jemima-never-pancakes/
https://en.wikipedia.org/wiki/Aunt_Jemima

*Kraft Singles*
https://recipes.howstuffworks.com/history-of-grilled-cheese.htm
https://en.wikipedia.org/wiki/Kraft_Singles

*SpaghettiOs*
https://en.wikipedia.org/wiki/SpaghettiOs
https://en.wikipedia.org/wiki/Franco-American_(brand)

*Pop-Tarts*
https://www.mashed.com/117295/untold-truth-pop-tarts/
https://en.wikipedia.org/wiki/Pop-Tarts
https://www.campbells.com/spaghettios/

*Space Food Sticks*
https://www.oldtimecandy.com/collections/walk-the-candy-aisle-space-food-sticks
https://flashbak.com/space-food-sticks-the-1970s-nasa-snack-to-plug-the-gap-40957/
http://spacefoodsticks.com/index.html

The following trademarks and registered trademarks are the property of their respective holders: Aunt Jemima, Beefaroni, Betty Crocker, Birdseye, Campbell, Chef Boy-ar-dee, Coca-Cola, Conagra, Country Squares, Franco-American, General Foods, Grapelade, Heinz, Hormel, Hunt's, Kellogg, Kraft, Kraft Singles, Log Cabin, Nabisco, NASA, Pepsi-Cola, Peter Pan, Pillsbury, Pop-Tarts, Post, Quaker Oats, Skippy, Smucker's, Smucker's Goober, Space Food Sticks, SpaghettiOs, SPAM, Swanson, Tang, Toastees, Toast-em Pop-Ups, Welch, Wonder Bread

# CHAPTER 6

# Toys, Games and Comic Books

In the 50s and 60s, every Boomer kid loved to play, and there were plenty of toys and games to play with. Younger children could play simple games like Candy Land with their parents, move Colorforms around on a special shiny surface, or dress Barbie dolls for hours on end. Older kids built stuff with LEGOs, Lincoln Logs and TINKERTOYS, and they spent a lot of time outside, riding Schwinn bikes, roller skating on sidewalks, throwing Frisbees, and hitting WIFFLE balls.

Many toys of the time were influenced by children's and family television shows. For example, the popularity of TV Westerns spawned cowboy hats, cap guns, and cowboy and Indian playsets. "Watch Mr. Wizard," the popular children's TV show, led kids to clamor for their own do-it-yourself science kits. Disney films and television shows created an entire genre of Disney-branded toys and games. Some fads, like the Hula Hoop, caught on and prevailed, while others, like troll dolls, sparked interest but flamed out quickly.

Board games were the video games of the era. Younger and older Boomer kids alike played them with friends and with the whole family. They were great for rainy days and road trips. Board games became more sophisticated as production techniques improved. So many games came to market in the 50s and 60s that they had to be classified by the appropriate age group. The popularity of board games continues to this day.

Parents encouraged their children to read, but they may have been less than enthusiastic about the favorite reading material of Boomer kids – comic books. Still, parents knew from their own childhood that comic books were a rite of passage. Popular in the 1930s and 1940s, comic books took on a whole new life in the 50s and 60s with the advent of television. The cross-over between television and comic book characters was significant, each medium benefitting from the other. Super-heroes weren't the only ones who shared both the small screen and printed page; such popular TV shows as "The Lone Ranger" and "Sea Hunt" inspired comic book series of their own.

Whether it was toys, games, or comic books, Boomer kids found many ways to amuse themselves and occupy their leisure time. Play time (*sans* computer or smartphone) was an integral part of growing up in the Boomer era.

## Barbie

Few toys have achieved the monumental success of "Barbie." Created by Ruth Handler and named after Barbara, her daughter, the doll was introduced by Mattel in 1959. "Ken," named after Handler's son Kenneth, came along in 1961. With Barbie, Mattel pioneered the use of aspirational advertising for a toy on television. In her very first commercial, Barbie (in brunette and blond versions) was featured in various outfits. The ad jingle ended with the lyric, "I'll make believe that I am you." Every girl wanted not just to own Barbie, but to *be* Barbie. Barbie was a true fashion doll; she had a controversial figure (breasts!) and a wardrobe that seemed endless. All of her clothing and accessories were sold separately. In the first year, some 350,000 Barbie dolls were sold, and to date, over one billion Barbies have been sold in 150 countries worldwide. Barbie has been a true franchise; it is by far Mattel's largest, most profitable line. In addition to a multitude of Barbie dolls and accessories, a wide range of Barbie branded merchandise is available, everything from books to cosmetics to video games and films.

Photo credit: Barbie box, Mike Mozart, TheToyChannel, Flickr.com, CC BY 2.0

## Cap Gun

The cap gun may seem sinister, but this toy reached the height of its popularity in the 50s and 60s. The cap gun was most often associated with a Western television show. Whether it was the long-barreled "Wyatt Earp Buntline Special," the derringer created by Mattel for the show "Yancy Derringer," or the toy version of the weapon used by "The Rifleman," Boomer kids (mostly boys) were likely to own at least one. Caps made the cap gun even more exciting by simulating the noise, smell, and smoke of a real gun. Essentially tiny fireworks, caps came individually, on rolls and on disks, designed to fit the specific cap gun. Once American parents started to witness the horrors of the Vietnam War on television, cap guns quickly lost their broad appeal as children's toys. I classify the cap gun as a loser for the reason that, quite simply, a gun is not a toy... and a toy should not be a gun. In addition, those little caps could be quite dangerous. I remember my friends and I playing with strips of caps, setting them off by striking them with rocks. In retrospect, not a smart move.

Photo credit: Dick toy cap gun, Joe Haupt, Flickr.com, CC BY-SA 2.0

## Comic Books

The "Golden Age" of comic books – when the modern comic book was born and flourished – occurred in the 1930s and 1940s. Indeed, that's when the Superman and Batman characters were introduced. This period was followed by the "Silver Age" from the 50s through the early 70s, when a slew of comic book brands such as Action, DC and later Marvel churned out superhero, crime, Western, science fiction, horror and even romance comic books. "Classics Illustrated" was one of the few high-brow series of comic books. Boomer kids were known to read comic books by flashlight under their sheets, much to their parents' chagrin. When the influence of comic books was investigated by Congress in 1954, the comic book industry instituted its own "Comics Code" which cleaned up comic book content for a while. Interestingly, a comic book called "MAD" was converted into a "magazine" to bypass the Code; it became highly successful. The Code was eventually abandoned. Comic books and comic book characters have witnessed a rebirth in recent years, in no small part thanks to nostalgia-hungry Boomers.

### ERECTOR Set

Was the "ERECTOR Set," introduced in 1913, responsible for turning kids into structural engineers? Not quite, but it did foster an interest in construction that influenced other toys such as "TINKERTOY" and "LEGO." Alfred C. Gilbert created the steel toy after he witnessed the erection of steel girders to carry power lines. It was immediately in vogue, especially due to the novelty of including a working motor. During World War II, the ERECTOR Set had to be manufactured of wood, but it was back to steel in the 50s. While remaining popular, the Gilbert ERECTOR Set was complex and unwieldly; some Boomer kids probably felt as if they *did* need an engineering degree to play with it. The antiquated design was unable to compete with more contemporary, easier to use plastic toys that came to market in the Boomer era. The A. C. Gilbert Company filed for bankruptcy in 1967. Still, ERECTOR would not die. The brand was sold a few times and today, it is owned by Meccano, the company that developed the UK's first construction set in 1898.

Photo credit: 1952 Gilbert Erector Set ad, Popular Mechanics magazine, Joe Haupt, Flickr.com, CC BY-SA 2.0

## Paint by Numbers

"Paint by Numbers" was a remarkable cross-over concept that delighted both adults and Boomer kids. Max Klein, owner of Palmer Paint Co., challenged employee Dan Robbins to find a way to sell more paint. Inspired by Leonardo da Vinci's method of numbering diagrams to teach painting, Robbins came up with the "paint by numbers" concept, introduced in 1951 under the "Craft Master" brand. It wasn't an immediate hit until folks figured out that they could make great-looking paintings with absolutely no talent. Robbins was a real idea man: One of his breakthrough promotions was to create a giant blank billboard of a paint-by-number scene. Bleachers were set up in front of the billboard so people could watch as, each day, another color was added. Paint-by-number kits became so popular that President Dwight D. Eisenhower bragged about the paintings he created to hang in the White House. By 1955, Palmer Paint had sold 20 million paint-by-number kits. During the height of their popularity, the kits included landscapes, buildings, cars, and every conceivable type of subject – even JFK, as seen above.

Photo credit: JFK Paint by Numbers, Larry Miller, Flickr.com, CC BY-SA 2.0

## Sea-Monkeys

Remember how fascinated you were with "Uncle Milton's Ant Farm"? Remember how disappointed you were with "Sea-Monkeys"? They were actually a weird kind of brine shrimp that remained in suspended animation until "released" by a proper mix of nutrients and chemicals. Working with a marine biologist, Harold von Braunhut invented and packaged a product that contained all the ingredients needed to create "instant life." In 1962, he named it "Sea-Monkeys" because he thought the brine shrimp tails resembled the tails of monkeys. This scientific toy featuring tiny crustaceans turned out to be a giant letdown. If and when the shrimp came alive, the "Sea-Monkeys" looked nothing like the cute cartoon monkey illustrations in ads, most of which appeared in comic books in the late 50s and 60s. The illustrations were inaccurate, and the ad's promise of "a bowlfull of happiness" could not have been further from the truth. Most Boomer kids and their parents saw "Sea-Monkeys" as nothing more than a scam. Still, they became a pop culture fad... and are still being sold today.

Photo credit: Sea-Monkeys, Cornellier, CC BY-SA 4.0

### Easy-Bake Oven

Kenner figured little girls would get excited if they could be just like mom, so in 1963, the toy maker introduced the realistic "Easy-Bake Oven." It allowed Boomer kids to safely bake up a storm – kind of. The oven ingeniously worked with two light bulbs to prevent burns. The Easy-Bake Oven was said to have been inspired by New York City street vendors, who kept pretzels warm under lights. Betty Crocker added her name to the product and made specially designed mixes that would "bake" in the provided pans via the light bulbs. The baked product was of questionable quality, but the concept was a smash. The oven was available in turquoise or yellow. Kenner and then Hasbro, which acquired Kenner, has sold more than 23 million of the ovens since its inception. The Easy-Bake Oven has been redesigned over the years to keep up with modern technology. Believe it or not, an updated version released in 2011 actually included a real heating element that could reach a temperature of 375 degrees. Hopefully today's kids will be careful with this new one!

Photo credit: Easy-Bake Oven package, BradRoss63, CC BY-SA 4.0

### Twister

Twister was originally conceived as a promotion for a shoe polish company by Reyn Guyer in 1964. Along with artist Charles Foley and toy designer Neil Rabens, Guyer came up with a game based on the promotion and called it "Pretzel." They sold the idea to game maker Milton Bradley, who renamed it "Twister" and introduced it in 1966. Twister probably never would have succeeded if it hadn't been for its placement on "The Tonight Show," where Johnny Carson played Twister with actress Eva Gabor. It had them contorted around one another in a steamy demonstration of just how the game was played. The game sold out the next day at the one New York store that stocked it. More than three million copies of Twister were sold in 1967. Twister seemed like a passing fad, and on that basis, it qualifies as a "loser." Also, after playing it, adults and kids alike probably needed to visit a chiropractor. Who knows, it may have also resulted in unwanted pregnancies. Despite all that, in a new twist, Twister resurfaced in the 1980s as a favorite of college students. Well well, the silliness lives on after all.

Photo credit: Twister game, CCO 1.0, public domain

### Mr. Potato Head

Mr. Potato Head started out as a real potato. Inventor George Lerner created face parts to stick into a potato and sold the idea as a premium to put in cereal boxes. Toy maker Hasbro (then called Hassenfeld Brothers) thought it had "po-tential" and marketed a kit of plastic pieces, with no potato, as "Mr. Potato Head" in 1952. "Mrs. Potato Head" came along in 1953. It was the very first toy to be advertised directly to children on television, starting a deluge of products targeting Boomer kids over the airwaves. The TV ads worked and over one million kits were sold in the first year. In 1964, to comply with government regulations banning sharp items in children's toys, a plastic body, accompanied by dull parts, was introduced. The modification didn't slow down sales; in fact, other characters were added to the Mr. Potato Head family. Mr. Potato Head famously relinquished his pipe during the 1987 "Great American Smokeout." A whole new generation of kids became familiar with Mr. Potato Head when he starred in the 1995 movie, *Toy Story*, as well as *Toy Story 2* in 1998.

Photo credit: Mr. Potato Head figure, Pixabay.com

## Slinky

"Slinky" was an accident. In 1943, Richard James, a mechanical engineer, was working on springs that could stabilize sensitive equipment on ships. When he accidentally knocked a spring off the shelf, he noticed that it "walked" instead of just falling. That gave him the idea for a toy which he and his wife Betty named Slinky. The couple started a company and James developed a machine that was able to coil 80 feet of steel wire into a two-inch spiral. Slinky didn't sell until Gimbels in Philadelphia demonstrated it during the 1945 Christmas season. Slinky was nationally advertised, and 100 million Slinkies were sold in the first two years. In the early 50s, other toys incorporating Slinky were created. Later, Slinky was updated and made out of plastic. Boomer kids were fascinated with this thing that could seemingly walk by itself downstairs, but there wasn't much else to do with it – although I seem to remember one of my science teachers making creative use of one in an experiment. Today, there is a whole line of Slinky toys available. Still, it's a fad whose time has passed.

Photo credit: First Slinky box, Mike Mozart, TheToyChannel, Flickr.com, CC BY 2.0

## Sources

*If you would like free access to a special webpage that includes all of the source links from this book, simply send your email address to: guidewordspub@gmail.com. In the subject line, type: WL Links. Your email will remain private and will not be shared or sold.*

*Barbie*
https://en.wikipedia.org/wiki/Barbie
https://barbie.mattel.com/en-us/about/history.html

*Cap Gun*
https://en.wikipedia.org/wiki/Cap_gun
https://www.globaltoynews.com/2017/09/cap-guns-an-appreciation-.html

*Comic Books*
https://the-artifice.com/history-of-comics/
https://en.wikipedia.org/wiki/Comic_book

*ERECTOR Set*
https://en.wikipedia.org/wiki/Erector_Set
https://www.toyhalloffame.org/toys/erector-set
http://www.meccano.com/

*Paint by Numbers*
https://www.paintbynumbermuseum.com/dan_robbins_intro
http://mentalfloss.com/article/55752/history-paint-numbers

*Sea-Monkeys*
http://mentalfloss.com/article/56755/16-amazing-facts-about-sea-monkeys
https://en.wikipedia.org/wiki/Sea-Monkeys

*Easy-Bake Oven*
https://www.toyhalloffame.org/toys/easy-bake-oven
https://en.wikipedia.org/wiki/Easy-Bake_Oven

*Twister*
https://www.toyhalloffame.org/toys/twister
https://en.wikipedia.org/wiki/Twister_(game)

*Mr. Potato Head*
https://en.wikipedia.org/wiki/Mr._Potato_Head
https://www.toyhalloffame.org/toys/mr-potato-head

*Slinky*
https://www.toyhalloffame.org/toys/slinky
https://en.wikipedia.org/wiki/Slinky

The following trademarks and registered trademarks are the property of their respective holders: Action Comics, Ant Farm, Barbie, Batman, Betty Crocker, Candy Land, Classics Illustrated, Colorforms, Craft Master, DC Comics, Disney, Easy-Bake Oven, ERECTOR, Frisbee, Hasbro, Hula Hoop, LEGO, Lincoln Logs, The Lone Ranger, MAD, Marvel, Mattel, Milton Bradley, Mr. Potato Head, Mr. Wizard, The Rifleman, Schwinn, Sea Hunt, Sea-Monkeys, Slinky, Superman, The Tonight Show, TINKERTOY, Toy Story, Twister, WIFFLE Ball

# Health, Beauty and Cigarettes

After World War II, America was undergoing post-war prosperity. With the rise of the middle class came new and better jobs, a suburban lifestyle, leisure time, and self-confidence.

Men and women sought to look good in the 50s. Men wore suits to work. Housewives wanted to be attractive when their husbands came home, so they got "dolled up" with makeup and a stylish hairdo. Lipstick was popular in the 1930s and 1940s, but after the war, as much as 90 percent of American women wore lipstick. Lipstick and makeup got a boost from Hollywood; starlets, who could now regularly be seen on screen in color instead of just black-and-white, were carefully observed by consumers anxious to mimic their cinematic look.

In the 50s, Revlon introduced no-smear lipstick and Maybelline popularized mascara. Other cosmetics companies, such as Elizabeth Arden, Estee Lauder and Max Factor, were top brand names. Clairol created a sensation with in-home hair color in 1956. In-home hair dryers and rollers encouraged salon-like hair styling, and Toni made home permanents a reality. Secret, the first deodorant designed for women, debuted. Crest, introduced in 1955, became the first toothpaste to combine cosmetics with cavity prevention. Avon's door-to-door cosmetics concept was so successful that the company had 100,000 Avon Representatives and $100 million in sales by 1957. At the same time, the African-American population was struggling with the definition of "beauty." The magazine for blacks, *Ebony*, began publishing in 1945. It carried ads for skin bleaching cream and hair straighteners.

The 60s marked a generational shift in beauty. Eyes became more dramatic and lips got paler. The mid 60s saw a transition to a freer, more natural look – for some women, that meant the absence of makeup. Boomer kids in the 60s may have favored a hip, refined look – or a hippie look.

Remarkably, cigarettes were deemed a legitimate part of 50s and 60s culture; smoking was even endorsed by doctors in 50s advertising. Cigarette brands were heavily advertised – and there were no health warnings about tobacco until 1965.

Just as in other brand categories, health and beauty brands were enjoying a growth spurt in the late 40s, 50s and 60s as American consumers focused squarely on themselves and their families. And families were growing. That's when Boomer kids came into the world (along with an innovation for Baby Boomer moms – mass-marketed disposable diapers).

Most of the health, beauty and cigarette brands targeted adults, but Boomer kids became well aware of them as they grew up and progressed through adolescence.

### Clairol

Traveling in Europe in 1931, American Joan Gelb and husband Lawrence discovered "Clairol," a new French hair color product. The Gelbs purchased it from a Paris company and started a business in New York to sell it. It wasn't an easy sell, because before the 1950s, coloring your hair was thought to be appropriate only for actresses and hussies. Clairol legitimized hair coloring when "Miss Clairol" was introduced in 1956. Miss Clairol was the first at-home hair color kit that could lighten, tint, condition and shampoo hair in one step. It was launched with the provocative advertising slogan, "Does she or doesn't she? Only her hairdresser knows for sure." (It was written by a woman.) Other brilliant advertising slogans, such as "Is it true blondes have more fun?" and "You're not getting older... you're getting better" followed in the 50s and 60s. Just three years since its founding, Clairol became the top U.S. hair coloring brand, and it has been innovating in the field ever since. Boomer kids were probably amazed to see that their moms' hair color changed overnight. Maybe husbands were too!

Photo credit: 1957 Miss Clairol ad, 1950sUnlimited, Flickr.com, CC BY 2.0

## Brylcreem

The hit show/movie, "Grease," made a definitive statement about men's hairstyles in the 50s. Oiling or greasing the hair was popular at the time, and you can thank "Brylcreem," one of the leading products of the 50s, for that look. Created in 1928 by a British firm, Brylcreem was formulated from water, mineral oil and beeswax. When that lovely concoction was applied to a man's hair... well, use your imagination! A television jingle turned Brylcreem into a household word:

"Brylcreem... a little dab'll do ya.

Brylcreem... you'll look so debonair.

Brylcreem... the gals'll all pursue ya,

They'll love to run their fingers through your hair!"

Chances are Boomer boys entering adolescence borrowed their dad's Brylcreem and took a little dab for themselves in the hope that girls would notice them. Brylcreem fell out of favor in the 60s, when men started wearing longer hair without the greasy look. But the product has made a comeback – along with the "dab" tag line – claiming to offer "the perfect amount of shine."

Photo credit: Brylcreem ad, 70023venus2009, Flickr.com, CC BY-ND 2.0

### Dove

"Dove" managed to do something pretty special: It turned an ordinary commodity, a bar of soap, into a health brand. Invented in 1957 by American chemist Vincent Lamberti for his employer, Lever Brothers (today known as Unilever), Dove developed a unique selling proposition. Unlike every other soap which tended to dry the skin, "Dove Beauty Bar" contained ingredients that moisturized and nourished the skin. During an era when makeup was extensively used and dry skin was a chronic problem, this approach resonated with women. It worked then and it works now; today, Dove is the best-selling soap brand in the U.S. In fact, Dove is a health and beauty super brand that has expanded far beyond that original bar of soap. Included under the Dove brand umbrella are skin cleansing, skin care, deodorant, and hair care products, as well as a "Dove Men + Care" product line. Dove has also played a role in bringing attention to "real" beauty in women with its 2004 worldwide "Campaign for Real Beauty" and "Self-Esteem Project," which celebrates the natural variation in women's bodies.

Photo credit: Dove soap, public domain

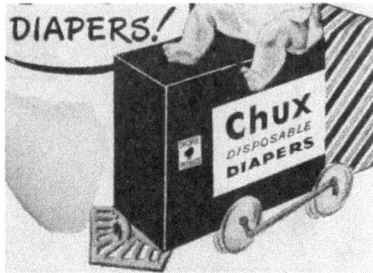

## Chux

What is something Boomer kids used a ton of without even knowing it? Diapers, of course. The Baby Boomer era created a crying need for cloth diapers and, later, a market for new-fangled disposable diapers. If you think "Pampers" was the first disposable diaper, think again. Another brand, Johnson & Johnson's "Chux," was actually the country's first mass-market disposable diaper. Introduced in 1935, Chux diapers were ahead of their time. The idea of disposable diapers hadn't yet caught on. They were more expensive than traditional cloth diapers – expensive enough to be a luxury rather than a necessity. In 1950, the prefold and snap-on pinless cloth diapers were invented, so diaper technology was advancing just fine without disposables. The Chux brand ran its course and disappeared. By the 60s, though, the time was right for disposable diapers – and along came "Pampers." Introduced by Procter & Gamble in 1961, Pampers became a national brand by 1969 and truly created the disposable diaper brand category.

Photo credit: Chux disposable diapers, image from an ad in *The Ladies' Home Journal*, public domain

## Crest

In the early 1940s, dental disease was a major problem in the U.S., with Americans suffering from about 700 million cavities each year. Toothpaste didn't help – it was designed to clean the teeth, not protect them. Procter & Gamble formed a research project to develop and test a new toothpaste containing fluoride. A clinical study showed an average 49 percent reduction in cavities in kids ages 6 to 16 who used the toothpaste. Adults benefitted nearly as much. This success led to the 1955 test marketing of "Crest with Flouristan" toothpaste, followed by a national rollout in 1956. The American Dental Association (ADA) endorsed Crest in 1960. Two years later, Crest had become the country's best-selling toothpaste. Early advertising often showed children exclaiming "Look Mom... no cavities!" The Crest brand has expanded since the toothpaste introduction into other oral healthcare products. Crest "Pro-Health" Toothpaste has received the ADA Seal of Acceptance for protection against six different dental health conditions.

Photo credit: 1958 Crest toothpaste ad, *Reader's Digest* magazine, SenseiAlan, Flickr.com, CC BY 2.0

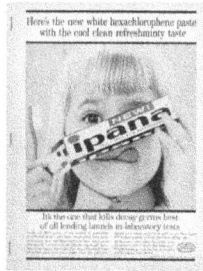

Here's the new white hexachlorophene paste with the cool clean refreshminty taste

It's the one that foils decay germs best of all leading brands in laboratory tests

## Ipana

Chances are Boomer kids would have chosen "Ipana" tooth-paste on the basis of "Bucky Beaver" alone. But before Bucky, this toothpaste brand, introduced by Bristol-Myers in 1901, was a hit on radio. Ipana sponsored radio programming featuring the "Ipana Troubadors," who became a renowned dance band in the 1920s. When Bristol-Myers wanted to grow market share (and compete with Crest), they turned to Disney in 1954, who created the "Bucky Beaver" character, voiced by none other than chief Mouseketeer, Jimmie Dodd. An animated Bucky sang and danced in television commercials and appeared in comic strip ads. The brand was also heavily advertised in women's maga-zines. Through the 60s, Ipana was a very well-known, popular toothpaste brand. In the 1970s, however, Bristol-Myers turned its attention to the more lucrative pharmaceuticals market, for the most part ignoring Ipana. It disappeared by the end of the decade. But wait: With the growing interest in retro brands, Ipana is making a comeback, thanks to the Canadian company, Maxill, which has acquired the brand, along with Bucky Beaver.

Photo credit: Ipana ad, Nesster on VisualHunt.com, CC BY

## Secret

People believed they needed to mask their body odor as early as 1888, the year "Mum" deodorant was trademarked. But "Secret," the first antiperspirant/deodorant created especially for women, didn't come along until 1956. Introduced by Procter & Gamble, Secret originally was available as a cream to be applied to the underarms. "Ice Blue Secret" roll-on followed in 1958. The first television commercial featured a woman dancing by the seashore in a willowy gown and voiceover that said, "To you, to every woman whose deodorant has ever failed her...comes new Ice Blue Secret." A spray was launched in 1964, and a solid stick version was introduced in 1978. Secret has been a model for the concept of brand extension, one of Procter & Gamble's strengths. The Secret brand now includes not just products, but "Collections," such as "Clinical Strength Protection," "Outlast Xtend Collection," "Active Collection," and "Fresh Collection." And every Secret product comes with a 60-day money-back guarantee. Now that's refreshing.

Photo credit: Excerpt from vintage Secret ad, twitchery, Flickr.com, CC BY 2.0

## Buster Brown Shoes

This brand qualifies as a "beauty" brand because of its impact on the appearance of Boomer kids. Older Boomers probably wore "Buster Browns" or "Mary Janes" as young children. George Brown founded the Brown Shoe Company in 1904, just two years after the appearance of "Buster Brown," a comic strip featuring Buster, his sweetheart Mary Jane, and his dog Tige. One of Brown Shoe Company's sales representatives got the idea to associate the comic strip character with the shoe brand. Until 1930, Brown Shoes were marketed using dwarf actors and dogs who made public appearances in stores and theaters. In the Boomer era, however, the shoe company ventured into comic book publishing. "Buster Brown Comics" were used to promote the shoe brand, and the image of Buster Brown and Tige appeared inside every shoe. The company also opened retail outlets. When Brown Shoes began to add other products to its line and fashions changed, Buster Browns and Mary Janes fell out of favor and walked off into the sunset.

Photo credit: Vintage Buster Brown clock, public domain

## Marlboro

If it weren't for a Boomer era advertising campaign, "Marlboro" may never have become the all-time leading cigarette brand. In the 1920s and 1930s, Philip Morris advertised Marlboro as a women's cigarette with the slogan, "Mild as May." The filter on the cigarette even had a printed red band around it, designed to hide red lipstick stains. By World War II, sales had suffered and other cigarette brands became more popular. To win back market share, it was decided that the brand should be repositioned to appeal to male smokers. In 1954, the "Marlboro Man" advertising campaign was introduced, featuring a number of rugged looking men, the most popular of which became a cowboy. He could be seen gallivanting in "Marlboro Country" in a subsequent campaign, which included print ads, outdoor billboards, and TV commercials with the theme song from the 1960 Western movie, "The Magnificent Seven." It was a national and eventually a worldwide blockbuster. The Marlboro brand was the leading cigarette brand in 1972 – and it has maintained that position ever since.

Photo credit: Marlboro cigarettes, Peyri Herrera, Flickr.com, CC BY-ND 2.0

MORE DOCTORS SMOKE CAMELS
THAN ANY OTHER CIGARETTE

## Camel

The lasting popularity of "Camel" cigarettes, a product of R. J. Reynolds, cannot be denied. So named because they contained Turkish tobacco, Camels have been a perennial favorite among smokers since their inception in 1913. Why, then, do I consider this brand a Boomer Brand "loser"? It's because of the brand's ignominious advertising history. During the late 40s and early 50s, R. J. Reynolds chose to position Camels as a healthy brand with advertising that claimed, "More doctors smoke Camels than any other cigarette." This statement was the result of surveys conducted by the cigarette company with doctors who had been given complimentary cartons of Camels. Even more notorious was the "Old Joe Camel" advertising campaign that ran from 1988 through 1997. This campaign, featuring a very cool-looking cartoon camel, was widely criticized for its insidious appeal to youngsters. A 1991 study indicated that over 91 percent of 6-year old kids could identify the character with cigarettes. That was almost the same result as associating Mickey Mouse with the Disney Channel. Shame on the Camel brand.

Photo credit: Camel ad, The U.S. Food and Drug Administration on VisualHunt.com

## Sources

*If you would like free access to a special webpage that includes all of the source links from this book, simply send your email address to: guidewordspub@gmail.com. In the subject line, type: WL Links. Your email will remain private and will not be shared or sold.*

*Health and Beauty Brands*

http://www.lipstickandcurls.net/blog/1950s-make-up-a-look-at-popular-beauty-brands-from-the-era

https://www.si.edu/spotlight/health-hygiene-and-beauty/make-up

https://glamourdaze.com/history-of-makeup

https://en.wikipedia.org/wiki/History_of_cosmetics

https://splinternews.com/a-look-back-at-4-decades-of-black-hair-and-beauty-ads-1793855531

https://www.collegefashion.net/beauty-and-hair/beauty-by-the-decade-the-1960s/

*Clairol*

https://www.clairol.com/en-US/inside-clairol

https://en.wikipedia.org/wiki/Clairol

*Brylcreem*

https://en.wikipedia.org/wiki/Brylcreem

https://www.brylcreemusa.com/#our-heritage

*Dove*

https://en.wikipedia.org/wiki/Dove_(toiletries)

https://www.unileverusa.com/brands/personal-care/dove.html

https://www.dove.com/us/en/home.html

https://www.statista.com/statistics/275244/us-households-most-used-brands-of-bar-soap/

*Chux*

https://ourstory.jnj.com/chux-disposable-diapers

https://www.diaperjungle.com/pages/history-of-diapers

https://en.wikipedia.org/wiki/Pampers

*Crest*
https://crest.com/en-us/oral-health/why-crest/faq/history-toothpaste

*Ipana*
http://www.buckybeaver.ca/ipana.php
http://www.maxill.com/ca/ipana

*Secret*
https://www.smithsonianmag.com/history/how-advertisers-convinced-americans-they-smelled-bad-12552404/
https://en.wikipedia.org/wiki/Secret_(deodorant_brand)
https://www.secret.com/en-us/collections

*Buster Brown Shoes*
https://americacomesalive.com/2016/06/20/buster-brown-shoes-mary-janes/
https://en.wikipedia.org/wiki/Buster_Brown#Brown_Shoe_Company_mascot

*Marlboro*
https://en.wikipedia.org/wiki/Marlboro_(cigarette)
https://en.wikipedia.org/wiki/Marlboro_Man

*Camel*
https://en.wikipedia.org/wiki/Camel_(cigarette)
http://tobacco.stanford.edu/tobacco_main/images.php?token2=fm_st138.php&token1=fm_img4072.php&theme_file=fm_mt015.php&theme_name=Targeting%20Teens&subtheme_name=Joe%20Camel

The following trademarks and registered trademarks are the property of their respective holders: American Dental Association, Avon, Brylcreem, Bucky Beaver, Buster Brown, Camel, Chux, Clairol, Crest, Crest Pro-Health, Disney, Dove, Dove Men + Care, Ebony, Elizabeth Arden, Flouristan, Ipana, Johnson & Johnson, Marlboro, Mary Janes, Maybelline, Max Factor, Maxill, Mickey Mouse, Miss Clairol, Mouseketeer, Pampers, Philip Morris, Procter & Gamble, R. J. Reynolds, Secret, Toni, Unilever

# Automobiles

In the 50s, Boomer kids grew up immersed in the new post-war car culture. The impact of the automobile during the Boomer era cannot be over-stated. The U.S. auto industry, the largest in the world, supported one in six American jobs. More than eight million cars were manufactured in 1950 alone, and more than sixty-seven million cars were registered in the U.S. by 1958.

During the 50s and 60s, Americans were crazy about cars. This is when NASCAR started, hot rods and drag racing went mainstream, and cruisin' the streets was the preferred teen evening and weekend activity.

American roads started to crisscross the country in 1955 thanks to the Interstate Highway System. With those roads came the birth of conveniences such as Holiday Inn motor inns and Howard Johnson restaurants, drive-in and drive-thru fast food restaurants, drive-in movie theatres, shopping malls and car washes. One third of the country's population lived in the suburbs by the end of the 50s.

Boomer kids and their parents commonly took extended summer road trip vacations. Driving across country was a popular pastime, as was camping in a pull-behind trailer.

The "Big Three" – Chrysler, Ford, and General Motors – dominated the marketplace, producing a dazzling array of car models, each a distinctive brand. Some were oriented towards families, while others were known as "muscle" cars, prized for their performance, power and speed. Cars ranged from the simple to the sublime. Sedans and station wagons were popular, as were expansive cars with outrageous tailfins. Vivid colors and chrome prevailed. New automotive advances such as automatic transmission, power brakes and power steering astonished and delighted drivers.

The Boomer era saw the advent of some truly legendary car brands, such as the Chevrolet Corvette, the Ford Mustang and the Pontiac GTO. There were also some clunkers, the most famous of which was the Ford Edsel. In the 60s, the Volkswagen Beetle and Microbus came to represent America's counter-culture movement.

Cars permeated popular culture: There were car magazines, television shows centered around cars, movies featuring car chases, books written about road trips and pop songs penned about cars.

The Boomer era will always be remembered as the time when Americans fell hopelessly in love with cars.

## 1957 Chevrolet

The '57 Chevy is today widely regarded as the most popular classic car in the world. Chevrolet had already achieved success the previous two years, but the 1957 model incorporated several design changes that made it even more attractive. Its unique features included a wide front grille with bumper "bullets," distinctive chrome headlights, tailfins, and a new dashboard. The wheels were one inch smaller in diameter – fourteen instead of fifteen inches – to make the car sit lower to the ground. It was the first car to have tubeless tires. Countless options were available, both in terms of body styles and accessories. The model came in 2- and 4-door sedans, a 2-door "Sport Coupe" and a 4-door "Sport Sedan," and several station wagon versions. Luxurious extras included power steering, power brakes, power windows, power seats, power antenna, rear speaker, padded dashboard, air conditioning, and even an electronic shaver that attached to the dashboard. The '57 Chevy was also a popular NASCAR and Daytona 500 competitor.

Photo credit: 1957 Chevrolet, Don O'Brien, Flickr.com, CC BY 2.0

## 1959 Cadillac

When it came to the 1959 Cadillac, beauty was in the eye of the beholder. This extraordinary-looking car had the most absurdly large tailfins imaginable. Cadillac pioneered tailfins eleven years earlier; supposedly, General Motors came up with the idea of tailfins after examining the rear stabilizers on a Lockheed airplane. By 1958, tailfins were a macho means of competition among automobile manufacturers, and Chrysler was said to be winning the fin war. Cadillac's designers didn't want that to happen. The tailfins on the '59 Cadillac were inspired by jet aircraft, but they were even more exaggerated due to a GM mass production mandate: The designers were required to use the same front door as a Buick. Since the door tapered to the rear, those outrageous fins, setting off twin bullet taillamps, were built up even higher. Hideous tailfins aside, the '59 Cadillac did have some redeeming qualities: The interior space was enormous, the wraparound windshield and side windows provided excellent visibility, and an automatic transmission, power steering and power brakes were all standard. Still, the '59 Cadillac is deserving of its reputation as a symbol of 1950s car kitsch.

Photo credit: 1959 Cadillac, Don O'Brien, Flickr.com, CC BY 2.0

## Ford Thunderbird

Iconic, classic, luxurious – all words that can be associated with the Ford Thunderbird, which got its name from a Native American supernatural, powerful bird. First introduced as a 2-seat convertible, the 1955 Ford Thunderbird (or "T-Bird") may have been designed to be a Chevy Corvette killer. Ford's competitive strategy worked: The Thunderbird did, in fact, outsell the Corvette in its early years. But the T-Bird was a different kind of car than the Corvette. With a rear seat added in 1958, the T-Bird was clearly positioned as more of a personal luxury automobile – a category pioneered by the Thunderbird – than a full-fledged sports car. The sporty yet luxurious Thunderbird evolved over several decades. It was upsized to include four-seat, five-passenger, and even six-passenger versions and then downsized back to its original 2-seat configuration until it went out of production in 2005. Regardless of size, however, Thunderbird was always luxurious, with many options available. And who can forget the girl who had "fun, fun, fun 'til her daddy took the T-Bird away," recorded by The Beach Boys in 1964.

Photo credit: Ford Thunderbird badge, CV Uribe, Flickr.com, CC BY 2.0

## Ford Edsel

September 4, 1957 – "E Day" – a day that will live in automotive infamy. That's the day the 1958 Ford Edsel was introduced to the American public amid great fanfare. It was one of the most extensively researched and most expensive car introductions. Ford even started a separate Edsel division in the hope that the new car would warrant its own production and sales operations. The Edsel, named after Edsel B. Ford, son of the company founder, was intended to compete with the Dodge and DeSoto models from Chrysler and the Buick, Oldsmobile and Pontiac brands from General Motors. According to Ford, the Edsel would be "the smart car for the younger executive or professional family on its way up." Unfortunately, also on the way up at the time was the growing popularity of compacts, combined with the waning interest in medium-priced cars. The massive publicity about the "car of the future" backfired: The Edsel was ridiculed instead of embraced for its less than attractive looks and the too-high price tag. Sales tanked. The Edsel remains one of the great brand disasters of the 20th Century.

Photo credit: Ford Edsel, Arend, Flickr.com, CC BY 2.0

## Pontiac GTO

The Pontiac GTO, introduced in 1964 by the Pontiac Motor Division of General Motors, is often credited as being the first "muscle car." One of its designers was John DeLorean, who went on to form his own car company in 1975. DeLorean named the Pontiac GTO after an Italian racing car designation; it stands for "Gran Turismo Omologato," but it's said that internally, the initials represented "Grand Tempest Option," since the car was originally conceived as a souped-up Tempest. The Pontiac GTO wasn't a true racing car, but it was sporty and had impressive performance because it was built with a larger engine – a 389-cubic inch V8 – in a lighter body. As soon as it was introduced and marketed, the Pontiac GTO was on its way to being a success, both in terms of sales and influencing other car brands to enter the muscle car market. By 1966, the Pontiac GTO broke away from the Tempest family to officially become its own model. The first Pontiac GTO era lasted ten years; the car was revived in 1999 as a concept car, but the brand was officially discontinued in 2009. Gone but not forgotten!

Photo credit: Pontiac GTO, pony rojo, Flickr.com, CC BY-SA 2.0

## Crosley Hotshot

The Chevrolet Corvette is considered America's first sports car, but it wasn't. That distinction goes to a car you may never have heard of – the Crosley Hotshot. Introduced in 1949, the Crosley Hotshot was a post-war sports car produced by a small automotive manufacturer, Crosley Motors, that specialized in building tiny, efficient cars since 1939. The initial Hotshot model was unique: It had two seats, no doors, no trunk lid (storage was accessed by folding down the seats), a low profile, all-wheel disc brakes, weighed around 1,000 pounds, and was priced at less than $1,000. Despite its size and economy, the Hotshot had impressive performance for its class and, when configured for racing, won its share of races. But it was destined to fail; once the larger Detroit automakers discovered that the sports car market was profitable, they started producing cars to compete with the Hotshot. After selling less than 2,500 of the diminutive cars, Crosley ended production in 1952. The Hotshot may have been the first American sports car, but it was short-lived.

Photo credit: 1950 Crosley Hotshot convertible, Jack Snell, Flickr.com, CC BY-ND 2.0

## Shelby Cobra

Where Crosley failed independently, Shelby succeeded by using a different strategy: Partnering with other manufacturers. A renowned race car driver, Carroll Shelby dreamed of building his own sports car. He got his opportunity when production of the AC Ace, a British sports car, ceased. Shelby contacted AC Cars, the manufacturer, and asked if he could create an American version by taking the lightweight Ace body and adding a more powerful V8 engine. When AC Cars agreed, Shelby worked a deal with Ford Motor Company to put their engine (first a 260 cubic inch and later a 289 cubic inch V8) in his new model, the "Shelby Cobra." The car was introduced in 1962 and immediately caught the eye of sports car enthusiasts. It was a formidable competitor in both domestic and international car races. Two years later, Shelby introduced a much more powerful version, the Cobra 427. It was this model for which the Shelby Cobra became legendary; the 427 could go from 0 to 100 mph in 10.3 seconds and remained America's fastest car for years. Today a Shelby Cobra is highly prized by car collectors.

Photo credit: Shelby Cobra, Rex Gray, Flickr.com, CC BY 2.0

## Amphicar

It's a car, it's a boat, it's Amphicar! The German-built Amphicar was introduced in America in 1961 as the first amphibious automobile. It was actually a descendant of the Volkswagen "Schwimmwagen," an amphibious vehicle that Nazi Germany used in World War II. While it was intended to appeal to Americans as a recreational vehicle, the Amphicar was expensive, unattractive, and viewed as nothing more than a novelty. In fact, the Amphicar was inadequate as both a car and a boat. It had a four-cylinder engine and manual transmission at a time when American engines were becoming more powerful and the popularity of automatic transmission was growing. Its speed on land could not exceed 70 mph; in water, the top speed was 7 knots. Front-wheel steering operated in the water and made it harder to navigate than a traditional boat. Lyndon Johnson owned an Amphicar, and he liked to scare the wits out of visitors to his ranch when he would drive it into a lake, claiming his brakes didn't work. Less than 4,000 Amphicars were manufactured, with production ending in 1965.

Photo credit: Amphicar, Greg Gjerdingen, Flickr.com, CC BY 2.0

## VW Beetle

The Volkswagen (VW) "Beetle" was conceived by German Ferdinand Porsche in 1933 at the request of Adolf Hitler, who wanted to build a "people's car" that all German citizens could afford. Because of World War II, civilian Beetles were not widely available until the end of the 1940s. The unusual (some would say ugly) looks and the rear-mounted engine were conversation starters, and the car became popular throughout Europe in the 50s – but not in the United States, where only 600 were sold in 1952. Also in the early 50s, the VW Microbus was introduced. A landmark advertising campaign in the U.S. that began in 1959 is generally credited with changing the American perception of the Beetle. Clever ads were focused on the quirkiness of the car, and the Beetle was quickly embraced as cool. In the 60s, the Beetle became the best-selling foreign car in the U.S. Both the hip Beetle and the economical "Microbus" were adopted by and associated with hippies. The Beetle was regarded as a "flower power bug," and the Microbus was seen as a live-in camper.

Photo credit: VW Beetle, Shadman Samee, Flickr.com, CC BY-SA 2.0

## Studebaker Lark

Studebaker built American cars as early as 1902. In 1933, the company went bankrupt, but it was rescued with the 1939 introduction of the popular Studebaker Champion. By the mid 50s, Studebaker was in trouble again. Known as "Studebaker-Packard" at that time, the company took a bold step to save itself: It abandoned full-size cars and, in 1959, produced one of the early compact cars in America, the Studebaker "Lark." Remarkably roomy – it could accommodate six passengers and luggage – the Lark was notably smaller and less ornate than the extravagant cars being manufactured by the Big Three. In the first two years, the Lark sold well; in fact, car dealers were willing to carry the Lark because Chrysler, Ford and General Motors did not offer compacts. The only real competition for the Lark came from the upstart American Motors Corporation (AMC), who offered the Rambler brand. By 1961, when the Big Three started to produce competing compacts, sales of the Lark plummeted as dealers dropped Studebaker. The Lark disappeared in 1964, and Studebaker went out of business in 1966.

Photo credit: 1959 Studebaker Lark, sv1ambo, Flickr.com, CC BY 2.0

## Sources

*If you would like free access to a special webpage that includes all of the source links from this book, simply send your email address to: guidewordspub@gmail.com. In the subject line, type: WL Links. Your email will remain private and will not be shared or sold.*

*Automobile Brands*
https://en.wikipedia.org/wiki/1950s_American_automobile_culture
https://gunthertoodys.com/1950s-car-culture/

*1957 Chevrolet*
https://en.wikipedia.org/wiki/1957_Chevrolet
http://www.classic-car-history.com/1957-chevy-history.htm

*1959 Cadillac*
https://www.100megsfree4.com/cadillac/cad1950/cad59s.htm

*Ford Thunderbird*
https://www.thecarconnection.com/news/1038521_the-iconic-ford-thunderbird-a-short-history-of-the-t-bird-from-1955--2005
https://en.wikipedia.org/wiki/Ford_Thunderbird

*Ford Edsel*
http://time.com/3586398/ford-edsel-history/
https://en.wikipedia.org/wiki/Edsel

*Pontiac GTO*
https://www.drivingline.com/articles/the-first-muscle-car-pontiac-gto-through-the-years/
https://en.wikipedia.org/wiki/Pontiac_GTO

*Crosley Hotshot*
https://www.hemmings.com/blog.article/the-little-car-that-could-1951-crosley-hotshot/
https://macsmotorcitygarage.com/americas-first-sports-car-the-crosley-hotshot/
https://en.wikipedia.org/wiki/Crosley

*Shelby Cobra*
https://www.hemmings.com/users/672028/story/2094.html
https://en.wikipedia.org/wiki/AC_Cobra

*Amphicar*
https://en.wikipedia.org/wiki/Amphicar

*VW Beetle*
https://en.wikipedia.org/wiki/Volkswagen_Beetle
http://www.classic-car-history.com/volkswagen-beetle-history.htm
https://www.popularmechanics.com/cars/trucks/a26207/volkswagen-microbus-vw-bus/

*Studebaker Lark*
https://en.wikipedia.org/wiki/Studebaker_Lark
https://ateupwithmotor.com/model-histories/studebaker-lark-super-lark/

The following trademarks and registered trademarks are the property of their respective holders: AC Ace, AMC, American Motors Corporation, Amphicar, The Beach Boys, Beetle, Buick, Cadillac, Chevy, Chevrolet, Chrysler, Cobra, Cobra 427, Corvette, Crosley, Crosley Hotshot, Dodge, Edsel, Ford, General Motors, GM,  Lark, Microbus, Mustang, NASCAR, Oldsmobile, Packard, Plymouth, Pontiac, Pontiac GTO, Rambler, Shelby Cobra, Studebaker, Tempest, Thunderbird, Volkswagen, VW

# CHAPTER 9

# Fast Food

The car culture of the 50s and 60s, in combination with convenience foods, created a new, powerful culinary movement in America: Fast food restaurants. That's why many major fast food restaurant chains began during the Boomer era.

"Fast food" may have really started with the novel concept of the Horn & Hardart Automat, popularized in New York City in 1912. Food was prepared in advance and put behind glass doors. Customers would select what they wanted by inserting coins and opening the doors to get their food. It was fast, but the concept didn't last.

When fast food restaurant chains came along, everything changed. At the beginning, the hamburger was king – even though neither Burger King nor McDonald's originated the fast food burger chain. White Castle was the first chain to serve up burgers in 1921 in a Wichita, Kansas storefront that looked like a small "white castle." The five-cent square "Sliders" were so popular they were sold by the sack. Soon, other White Castle locations followed, and a fast food hamburger chain was born.

Things really got rolling after World War II. That's when the car culture took over and burger joints began springing up like so much crab grass. By the 50s, fast food hamburger chains and franchises, both drive-ins and drive-thrus, dotted America's highways and byways. There were winners in the 50s and 60s, like McDonald's, Burger King and Wendy's, and losers like Burger Chef, Wetson's and White Castle copycat White Tower.

A burger-fries-soft drink fast food meal was heavenly sustenance to most Boomer kids. Mom may not have been particularly happy about it, though.

Boomer kids couldn't live on burgers alone, so fast food chains that served different cuisine started to open. Arby's, Chick-fil-A, Domino's, Dunkin' Donuts, Kentucky Fried Chicken, Little Caesar, Pizza Hut, Subway and Taco Bell all got their start in the 50s and 60s.

From a branding perspective, fast food restaurants were, and still are, marketing masters. They excel at the challenging task of branding an entire chain of restaurants, not just a single product. Their brand identity, menu, service, convenience and affordability remain remarkably consistent from one location to the next – and that's not easy to do. Many of the chains that launched in the Boomer era are still in business today. Whether or not you're a fan of fast food, you have to admire the "QSR" (Quick Service Restaurant) category for its brand acumen.

### Burger King

It's harder to be #2 than #1. Just ask Burger King, which has been trying to best the top burger chain, McDonald's, since 1953. Founded in Jacksonville, Florida as "Insta-Burger King" by Keith Kramer and Matthew Burns, the chain made use of an "Insta-Broiler" to differentiate its flame broiled hamburgers from McDonald's. In 1959, the partners sold the company to Miami franchisees James McLamore and David Edgerton, who renamed the company Burger King. The chain expanded to more than 250 locations before it was sold in 1967 to the Pillsbury Company. Decades of different ownership, management changes and quality issues with franchisees ensued. Despite all its ups and downs, Burger King remained solidly second to McDonald's, but in recent years, the chain ceded second place to Wendy's. The two firms continue to go back and forth, trading second and third place positions behind McDonald's. Today, Burger King has over 12,000 locations worldwide.

Photo credit: Burger King sign, Mike Mozart, TheToyChannel, Flickr.com, CC BY 2.0

## Burger Chef

Burger King needed a hamburger broiler, and to get it, they went to General Restaurant Equipment, a company owned by brothers Frank and Donald Thomas. The Thomas brothers saw the potential in the hamburger business and decided to open a few restaurants in Indianapolis to compete with Burger King. By 1958, the Thomas brothers, along with partner Robert Wildman, had stores in three states under the name "Burger Chef." They started a franchise operation using broilers built by their own General Restaurant Equipment company. Burger Chef came up with the modern hamburger meal, charging 45 cents for the "Triple Threat," a burger-fries-soft drink combination. By the end of 1967, Burger Chef was second only to McDonald's. It wouldn't last. General Foods acquired Burger Chef in 1968 and things started to fall apart soon after. The rapid expansion was halted. Burger Chef still had 800 stores in the late 1970s, but it was sold to Hardee's in 1982. The brand made a cameo appearance in an episode of the popular TV series, "Mad Men."

Photo credit: Burger Chef, Northridge Alumni Bear Facts, Flickr.com, CC BY-SA 2.0

## Chick-fil-A

Chick-fil-A didn't open until 1967, but its founder got started in 1946. That's when S. Truett Cathy opened a restaurant called "Dwarf House" in Georgia. Paradoxically, it served hamburgers and steaks. It wasn't until 1961 that Cathy discovered a pressure-fryer that could cook a chicken sandwich just as quickly as a hamburger. He served it at the Dwarf House but registered the name "Chick-fil-A," a play on "chicken fillet" that also meant "grade A" chicken. It took another six years before the first Chick-fil-A officially opened in an Atlanta suburb in 1967. While Kentucky Fried Chicken may have pioneered fried chicken, it was Chick-fil-A that created the fried chicken sandwich. The chain has grown rapidly through franchising. It has a relatively small number of restaurants in the U.S. (under 2,500), but the Chick-fil-A brand reportedly sells more per restaurant than any other American fast food chain – even McDonald's. It also has some of the friendliest employees – maybe because it hands out college scholarships to them like chicken sandwiches. Still, you can't find one open on a Sunday... that is the corporate policy.

Photo credit: Chick-fil-A, ccPixs.com, Flickr.com, CC BY 2.0

## Horn & Hardart

Horn & Hardart, opened by Joseph Horn and Frank Hardart, is heralded as the first true fast food chain in the country. The partners launched a location in Philadelphia in 1902, followed by one in New York City in 1912. The "Automat," as it was known, created a downtown sensation through the 50s. The most unusual aspect of the Automat was its futuristic service. To get cold food, customers would first turn in their cash for nickels. They would then pick the food they wanted, which appeared behind glass doors, and insert their nickels into coin slots. The door would open to reveal freshly made food. The food was cheap and good, and the system was perceived to be sanitary. Hot food was served at steam tables, and the eatery became known for its drip coffee. Horn & Hardart Automats grew to eventually be the largest restaurant chain in the world, serving some 800,000 diners daily. When fast food became more road-oriented, though, the concept faltered. Still, Horn & Hardart hung on until filing for bankruptcy in the 1990s. A company is now reviving the name as a brand of coffee.

Photo credit: Horn & Hardart postcard, Sean, Flickr.com, CC BY-ND 2.0

## Dunkin' Donuts

In 1948, William Rosenberg began selling donuts for five cents each and premium coffee for ten cents a cup at a restaurant in Quincy, Massachusetts. He named it "Open Kettle," but came up with the catchier "Dunkin' Donuts" in 1950. He said he wanted to "make and serve the freshest, most delicious coffee and donuts quickly and courteously in modern, well-merchandised stores." Clearly Rosenberg was on to something; he franchised the idea in 1955 and by 1965, over 100 stores had opened. While donuts have remained part of the name, the fast food chain has expanded into other baked goods, breakfast sandwiches, and more. It has also become known for its coffee, which has consistently inspired loyal customers for decades. Dunkin' Donuts has grown rapidly through franchising, as well as dramatically expanding through the acquisition of "Mister Donut" stores in 1990. Dunkin' Donuts now has more than 12,000 locations in 45 countries. The company reportedly serves close to two billion cups of hot and iced coffee annually.

Photo credit: Dunkin' Donuts sign, Mike Mozart, TheToyChannel, Flickr.com, CC BY 2.0

## LUM'S

The hamburger wasn't the only American classic – there was also the hot dog. LUM'S served them steamed in beer. Brothers Stuart and Clifford Perlman bought a hot dog stand called LUM'S in Miami in 1956. After opening four locations in five years, the Perlmans decided to franchise LUM'S. It was a hot idea – so hot that, by 1969, the company appeared on the New York Stock Exchange. LUM'S had grown to 400 locations when the Perlmans decided to invest in Caesars Palace in Las Vegas, betting $60 million it would work out. It did, and they soon ditched the hot dogs; in 1971, John Brown, then chairman of Kentucky Fried Chicken, bought LUM'S. He added other menu items, such as the "Ollieburger," and the chain began to offer international beer. Unfortunately for LUM'S, fried chicken was outselling hot dogs and beer, so in 1978, Brown sold the company to the owners of a chain called Wienerwald. In five years, that company was bankrupt, but a few remaining LUM'S operated independently. The last LUM'S, located in Bellevue, Nebraska, closed in 2017.

Photo credit: LUM'S, Ft. Lauderdale, FL, Florida Memory, Flickr.com

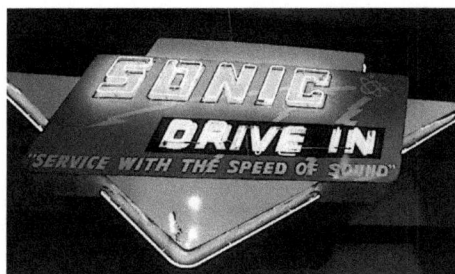

## SONIC

Only a handful of fast food restaurant chains were true "drive-ins" – restaurants that specialized in serving customers in their cars. This may seem like the ultimate in laziness (and it is), but in the context of the crazy car culture of the 50s and 60s, it makes perfect sense. After all, why get out of your beloved car when a carhop will come over and serve you? The country's first known drive-in was the Dallas, Texas establishment, Kirby's Pig Stand, which opened in 1921. Up until the 50s, drive-ins tended to be small operations. In 1953, Troy Smith Sr. purchased a root beer stand named "Top Hat" in Shawnee, Oklahoma. When traveling in Louisiana, Smith came across a drive-in that used speakers to take orders, which were then delivered to the cars. He liked the idea, so he converted Top Hat to the drive-in concept, building an intercom system and boasting the slogan, "Service at the Speed of Sound." It only seemed natural to change the restaurant's name to SONIC in 1959. Since then, SONIC has positioned its brand as "America's Drive-In," and it now has more than 3,500 locations in 44 states.

Photo credit: SONIC Drive-in neon sign, Kevin, Flickr.com, CC BY 2.0

## BONANZA and PONDEROSA

As mentioned in the first chapter, "Bonanza" was an incredibly popular Western, enjoying a fourteen-year run on TV. Dan Blocker was a big guy whose character was appropriately named "Hoss" on the show. Dan liked steaks – so he decided to horse around in the fast food business. Leveraging the success of the show, he opened a "Bonanza Steakhouse" in 1963 in Westport, Connecticut. It became a small chain and was purchased three years later by brothers Sam and Charles Wyly. They grew the chain to about 600 locations before they sold it in 1989. Just two years after Blocker opened his steakhouse, Dan Lasater, Norm Wiese and Charles Kleptz founded the similar "Ponderosa Steakhouse," whose name was based on the fictional ranch in the television show. Both chains competed head-to-head and grew. Proving truth is stranger than fiction, Bonanza and Ponderosa Steakhouses later ended up being sold to the same company, but they retained their individual identities. When the Western steakhouse concept got tired, the company went belly up. Most Bonanza and Ponderosa locations are gone.

Photo credit: Ponderosa Steakhouse sign, BillboardMister, CC BY-SA 3.0

## SUBWAY

In 1965, nuclear physicist Dr. Peter Buck wanted to help out college student Fred DeLuca with a way to pay his tuition. Buck loaned DeLuca $1,000 to open a sandwich shop in Bridgeport, Connecticut, which DeLuca named "Pete's SUBWAY" in Buck's honor. They served up fresh, affordable sub sandwiches, so popular that, by 1974, Buck and DeLuca owned and operated sixteen shops throughout Connecticut. They formed "Doctor's Associates" as an operating company and began franchising the concept under the name SUBWAY. The franchise has achieved unequalled success: Today, SUBWAY is the largest submarine sandwich chain in the world, spending more on U.S. advertising than any other fast food chain except McDonald's. There are more than 40,000 locations worldwide; more than half of them are in the United States. SUBWAY continues to specialize in freshly made sandwiches, baking its own bread in each location. It has also expanded into wraps, paninis, salads, breakfast sandwiches and a variety of baked goods.

Photo credit: SUBWAY sign, Mike Mozart, TheToyChannel, Flickr.com, CC BY 2.0

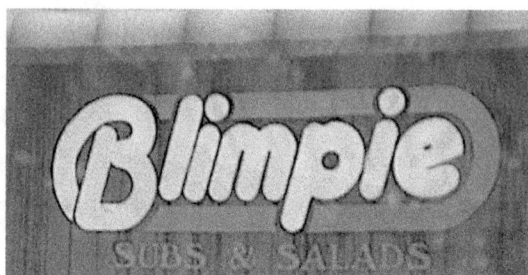

## Blimpie

Two leading submarine sandwich chains – Blimpie and Jersey Mike's – got their start in New Jersey. High school friends Tony Conza, Peter DeCarlo and Angelo Baldassare saw the business Mike's was doing and thought they could do just as well in their city of Hoboken. They opened a sub shop there in 1964. They wanted a word different from "sub" or "hoagie" in the name. A "blimp" was similar in shape and size to their stuffed sandwiches, so "Blimpie" was born. Baldassare left soon after the store's opening, but Conza and DeCarlo continued and grew the business by franchising on the East Coast. In 1976, they agreed to split the company in two. Conza retained control of the original Blimpie and expanded into the South. But in the 1980s, Conza got distracted by opening other restaurants. This allowed SUBWAY to grow their chain without much competition. Over the years, the company has always tried to compete with SUBWAY, managing to increase sales now and then. In recent years, however, Blimpie has been sold twice and has closed over 1,000 stores.

Photo credit: Blimpie sign, Doug Tammany, Flickr.com, CC BY-SA 2.0

## Sources

*If you would like free access to a special webpage that includes all of the source links from this book, simply send your email address to: guidewordspub@gmail.com. In the subject line, type: WL Links. Your email will remain private and will not be shared or sold.*

*Fast Food*
https://en.wikipedia.org/wiki/Fast_food_restaurant

*Burger King*
https://en.wikipedia.org/wiki/Burger_King

*Burger Chef*
https://jsfburgerchef.homestead.com/BurgerChefHistory.html
http://time.com/104799/burger-chef-mad-men-history/

*Chick-fil-A*
https://www.entrepreneur.com/article/311452
https://en.wikipedia.org/wiki/Chick-fil-A

*Horn & Hardart*
https://www.smithsonianmag.com/arts-culture/meet-me-at-the-automat-47804151/
https://dailycoffeenews.com/2017/08/01/iconic-american-automat-brand-horn-hardart-is-back-with-a-coffee-focus/

*Dunkin' Donuts*
https://en.wikipedia.org/wiki/Dunkin%27_Donuts
https://www.dunkinbrands.com/brands/dunkin-donuts

*LUM'S*
https://en.wikipedia.org/wiki/Lum%27s
https://www.omaha.com/go/dining/last-lums-restaurant-closes-after-years-in-bellevue-chain-had/article_44bffe00-4641-11e7-bfae-fb0d634d483c.html

*SONIC*
https://corporate.sonicdrivein.com/history/

https://en.wikipedia.org/wiki/Sonic_Drive-In

*Bonanza and Ponderosa*
https://en.wikipedia.org/wiki/Ponderosa_and_Bonanza_Steakhouses
https://www.usatoday.com/story/money/business/2012/12/12/restaurants-skrinking-business-bennigans/1764595/

*SUBWAY*
https://en.wikipedia.org/wiki/Subway_(restaurant)
https://www.subway.com/en-US/AboutUs/History

*Blimpie*
http://mentalfloss.com/article/72645/10-things-you-might-not-know-about-blimpie

The following trademarks and registered trademarks are the property of their respective holders: America's Drive-In, Arby's, Automat, Blimpie, Bonanza, Burger Chef, Burger King, Caesars Palace, Chick-fil-A, Coca-Cola, Coke, Domino's, Dunkin' Donuts, Dwarf House, General Foods, Hardees, Horn & Hardart, In-N-Out, Jack in the Box, Kentucky Fried Chicken, Little Caesar's, LUM'S, Mad Men, McDonald's, New York Stock Exchange, Open Kettle, Pizza Hut, Ponderosa, Service at the Speed of Sound, SONIC, SUBWAY, Taco Bell, Top Hat, Wendy's, Wetson's, White Castle, White Tower, Winerwald

# Rock 'n' Roll

With this chapter, we move into the late 60s and early 70s. We also begin to dramatically expand the concept of branding. Until now, the brands we've been discussing have been things – television shows, products of one kind or another, and fast food chains. These are tangible – we watched, bought, or visited them. Now we will define a "brand" more broadly as a music genre, a song, and even a performer. Stick with me and you'll see where I'm going.

I think we can all agree that "rock 'n' roll" is a very distinct kind of music that got its start during the Boomer era. While its roots are complex, it emerged with a bang in the 50s and 60s, much to the delight of Boomer kids and to the dismay of our parents. A radio disc jockey, Alan Freed, is credited with originating the name "rock 'n' roll." Guess what – that's branding!

If you accept the notion that "rock 'n' roll" is a brand, you could probably accept that sub-genres – folk rock, acid rock, hard rock, the "Motown sound," etc. – are sub-brands. And it certainly isn't a stretch to view every song within a genre as a distinct brand of its own.

When Boomer kids were growing up, we listened endlessly to particular songs. Each song had a special meaning for us and evoked emotions. It had lyrics we remember to this day. Each special song made a permanent imprint on us – and that's exactly what a great brand does.

You can say the same thing about the artists who recorded those songs. They were "personal brands." We had our favorite performers. We may have attended their concerts, belonged to their fan clubs, or bought merchandise with their names on it. Some performers were so famous, they were known by a single name ("Elvis" or "Dylan," for example).

Rock bands were great marketers. Whether it was "The Beach Boys" or "The Beatles," we recognized their names and their music because they were memorable brands. Those of us who delved deeper into music, and maybe play instruments ourselves, know that musicians use notable brands associated with rock music (such as Rickenbacker guitars, Moog synthesizers, Vox amplifiers, Yamaha keyboards, Zildjian cymbals).

Are rock Boomer Brands sustainable? You bet they are. How else do you explain the popularity of aging rockers Paul McCartney, The Rolling Stones, The Eagles and others who still perform at sold out worldwide tours.

The birth of the rock 'n' roll brand will always be inextricably linked with the Boomer era, as will rock songs, rock performers, and rock festivals. Rock 'n' roll is a brand of music that is uniquely ours.

## "American Pie"

The youngest Boomer kids were already seven years old when Don McLean's "American Pie" came out in 1971, but this one song is so emblematic of the Boomer era that it is worthy of designation as a Boomer Brand "winner." A sweeping poetic anthem, "American Pie" laments the loss of rock 'n' roll stars Buddy Holly, Ritchie Valens and "The Big Bopper" (J.P. Richardson), who were killed in a Feb. 3, 1959 plane crash. Because of McLean's song, that date became known as "the day the music died." Other lyrics are more obscure; over the years, McLean has refused to explain them, but in 2015, when the song's manuscript went up for auction, he offered at least a glimpse of context. The theme of the song is connected to America's loss of innocence from the late 50s to the late 60s. McLean said, "things are heading in the wrong direction. It is becoming less ideal, less idyllic. ... it is a morality song in a sense." Whatever the interpretation, the song was #1 for four weeks on U.S. charts in 1972, and it was ranked the #5 "Song of the Century."

Photo credit: American Pie album, Kenneth Hagemeyer, Flickr.com, CC BY-ND 2.0

## "Eve of Destruction"

"American Pie" was lyrical and elegiac, but the 1965 protest song, "Eve of Destruction," was plodding and angry. Recorded in a raspy voice by Barry McGuire, formerly of the New Christy Minstrels, the song met with controversy as soon as it was released. Some radio stations refused to play it because it was anti-government; in fact, "Eve of Destruction" was banned by Radio Scotland and put on BBC's "restricted" list. This very reaction to the song increased the intrigue surrounding it. When first issued, "Eve of Destruction" didn't even make the Top 100 in the U.S., but the negative media frenzy helped catapult it to #1 eventually, both in the U.S. and Canada. Still, the 19-year old songwriter, P. F. Sloan, along with McGuire, could never shake the controversy. According to Sloan, "The media headlined the song as everything that is wrong with the youth culture. ... I told the press it was a love song. A love song to and for humanity, that's all. It ruined Barry's career as an artist and in a year I would be driven out of the music business too."

Photo credit: An atomic explosion transfixed over a sunset in the Dominican Republic, Gaspard, Flickr.com, CC BY 2.0

### The Beach Boys

Formed in 1961, "The Beach Boys" created the California sound and became one of the most influential and resilient rock bands in America. The original band consisted of brothers Brian, Dennis and Carl Wilson, along with cousin Mike Love and friend Al Jardine. Early songs concentrated on surfing, sun, cars and girls; however, the influential 1966 album, "Pet Sounds," and the single, "Good Vibrations," proved the band could rise above their teen roots and evolve into a musical powerhouse. They sustained their popularity even during the 1964 "British Invasion." Despite band personnel changes and the progression of rock music, The Beach Boys have managed to accumulate thirty-six Top 40 songs in the U.S. between the 60s and 2010, more than any other American rock band. Over that same period, over eighty of their songs have made worldwide charts, and the band has sold more than 100 million records worldwide. The Beach Boys continue to tour today.

Photo credit: Best of the Beach Boys 1, Ed, Flickr.com, CC BY 2.0

### Jan & Dean

Rock duo Jan & Dean (William Jan Berry and Dean Ormsby Torrence) were best known for their copycat sound of The Beach Boys. Not only were they influenced by the band, Brian Wilson of The Beach Boys and Berry collaborated on about a dozen songs, including "Surf City," one of their biggest hits in 1963. During the duo's peak years of 1963 – 1964, they also released "Drag City," "Dead Man's Curve," and "The Little Old Lady from Pasadena," all of which made the Top Ten. They performed in *The T.A.M.I Show,* a 1964 concert film featuring major rock acts, and filmed two television pilots, neither of which were released. Once the surfin' sound subsided, Jan & Dean were never able to match their earlier success. They tried their hand at musical parody; their 1966 album, "Jan & Dean Meet Batman," included unfortunate, forgettable novelty songs, such as "The Origin of Captain Jan & Dean the Boy Blunder." After Berry had a serious car accident in 1966, the duo stopped performing. They attempted a comeback in the 1970s and later toured individually until Jan Berry died in 2004.

Photo credit: Jan & Dean, 1964, WWDC Radio, public domain

## The British Invasion

In 1963, a British group named "The Beatles" released their first U.S. single, "Please Please Me." It was the official kick-off of "Beatlemania" that swept not just the U.S. but the world. The Beatles spearheaded the mid 60s "British Invasion" in America. Ironically, British rock groups were basically adding their own accent to American rock 'n' roll music and playing it back to Americans. Boy were we buying it – not just the music, but the hair and clothing styles as well. Mop top cuts on guys, the Mod look, miniskirts and Twiggy were all in. Once the musical doors opened, they couldn't be closed: We welcomed British band brands such as the Animals, the Dave Clark Five, the Hollies, the Kinks, the Rolling Stones, the Who, the Yardbirds and the Zombies onto our shores. At the top of the pile was The Beatles, who would take over American news, television, the concert circuit, and rock charts. John, Paul, George and Ringo were the world's most celebrated rock stars, and the "fab four" went on to become the greatest band in rock history.

Photo credit: The Beatles – England, julio zeppelin, Flickr.com, CC BY-ND 2.0

## Novelty Songs

One thing you can say about Boomer kids – we had a quirky sense of humor. Whether it was practical jokes, comic books or MAD magazine, we liked to laugh. It was only natural that the music industry would find a way to appeal to our more jovial side with a brand of music called "novelty songs." Some of them caught on and some of them bombed. Many of them were juvenile and in poor taste, none more than the 1966 embarrassment, "They're Coming to Take Me Away, Ha-Haaa!" by Napoleon XIV, which crudely ridiculed the mentally ill. The 50s gave rise to such wild and crazy classics as "The Purple People Eater" (Sheb Wooley), "The Flying Saucer" (Buchanan and Goodman), "The Blob" (The Five Blobs), "The Chipmunk Song" (David Seville) and "Kookie, Kookie, Lend Me Your Comb" (Edward Byrnes and Connie Stevens). Not to be outdone, the 60s had its share of silly spoofs, including "Mr. Custer" (Larry Verne), "Monster Mash" (Bobby "Boris" Pickett), "The Surfin' Bird" (The Trashmen), "Snoopy vs. The Red Baron" (The Royal Guardsmen) and "Leader of the Laundromat" (The Detergents).

Photo credit: Juke box, France 1978 on VisualHunt.com, CC BY-SA

### The Byrds

If it weren't for The Beatles, The Byrds may never have gotten their start in California in 1964. Both Roger McGuinn, who was writing songs for other performers at the time, and Gene Clark, who was with the New Christy Minstrels, were enamored of the British group, and that's what first brought them together as a duo. McGuinn and Clark added David Crosby (who later went on to form Crosby, Stills, Nash and Young), and then Chris Hillman and Michael Clarke came on board to create The Byrds. Their very first record, "Mr. Tambourine Man," (1965) made it to #1. More importantly, the song represented the band's unique blend of folk music and the British sound. A number of Bob Dylan songs recorded by The Byrds cemented their legacy as the pioneers of "folk rock." Later, though, they transitioned into such genres as psychedelic rock, raga rock and country rock. By early 1969, band members flew the coop until McGuinn was the sole Byrd left. McGuinn reconstituted The Byrds with new musicians, but in 1973, he returned with the original members for a reunion album – their final one as a group.

Photo credit: The Byrds Greatest Hits, Piano Piano!, Flickr.com, CC BY 2.0

## "Louie Louie" by The Kingsmen

The lyrics are unintelligible. The musicianship is amateurish. The lead singer screws up a verse. The drummer drops a stick about a minute into the song and yells an obscenity. The quality of the record is so awful it sounds like it was produced in a parking lot. Oh, and it's recorded in one take. That pretty much sums up "Louie Louie," a one-hit wonder by an unknown Portland, Oregon band called "The Kingsmen" recorded in 1963. Remarkably, the record was a big hit. Why? Because "Louie Louie" was said to have dirty lyrics... so dirty that the FBI had agents follow the young band around on tour to see if they could identify obscene words. Turns out all they heard was the same garbled mumbo-jumbo lead singer Jack Ely sang on the record. Rebuffed, the FBI dropped their investigation, but that only increased the song's popularity. The lyrics, written by Richard Berry, never were dirty – but the "Louie Louie" mythology lives on. There have been parades and festivals in honor of the song, and there is even an "International Louie Louie Day" celebrated every year on April 11.

Photo credit: Photo of The Kingsmen, 1966, Scandore/Shayne personal management, public domain

## Soul Train

"Soul Train," a music and dance television program targeting African-American teens, did not appear nationally until 1971, but its roots go back to 1965 dance programs that aired on a Chicago TV station. Those programs opened the door for Don Cornelius, a news reporter for the station who also held "record hops" at local high schools. He called them "The Soul Train" and turned his concert series into a television show. The show was clearly influenced by the popular TV show "American Bandstand" (highlighted in the book, *BOOMER BRANDS*). Hosted by Cornelius, Soul Train was nationally syndicated from late 1971 until 2006 and featured a range of musical styles, including funk, pop, R&B, soul and later, disco and hip hop. The inception of the show was at a time when black consciousness was being raised in America. Not only were Soul Train's host, performers and studio audience black, the television commercials supporting the show were designed to appeal to a predominantly black audience – a rarity at the time.

Photo credit: Soul Train photo exhibition at Expo 72, Daniel X. O'Neil, Flickr.com, CC BY 2.0

### Shindig!

"Shindig!" was an ABC television weekly music variety show created and hosted by a Los Angeles disc jockey, Jimmy O'Neill. It was actually a 1964 replacement for the show "Hootenanny," a folk music show whose popularity plummeted as British rock took over the teen music scene. Shindig! covered a broad range of popular music and featured American pop stars of the day, such as Sam Cooke, The Everly Brothers and The Righteous Brothers, all of whom appeared on the first episode. Shindig! also did an admirable job of exposing British talent to an American audience – The Beatles, the Rolling Stones and the Who were among the performers who appeared on the show. Shindig! is credited with influencing the creation of other teen music shows, such as "Hollywood a Go Go," "Hullabaloo," and "Shivaree." The star power of Shindig! couldn't save it in the long run, though; it lasted less than two years. In 1965, the one-hour evening show was split into two half-hour programs that ran on two different nights, and it was cancelled in January 1966. The show that replaced it was the campy "Batman."

Photo credit: Photo of Jimmy O'Neill, host of Shindig, ABC Television, public domain

## Sources

*If you would like free access to a special webpage that includes all of the source links from this book, simply send your email address to: guidewordspub@gmail.com. In the subject line, type: WL Links. Your email will remain private and will not be shared or sold.*

*"American Pie"*
https://en.wikipedia.org/wiki/American_Pie_(song)
https://people.com/celebrity/don-mclean-talks-american-pie-song-meaning-before-manuscript-auction/

*"Eve of Destruction"*
https://www.songfacts.com/facts/barry-mcguire/eve-of-destruction
https://en.wikipedia.org/wiki/Eve_of_Destruction_(song)

*The Beach Boys*
https://en.wikipedia.org/wiki/The_Beach_Boys
https://www.rockhall.com/inductees/beach-boys

*Jan & Dean*
https://en.wikipedia.org/wiki/Jan_and_Dean

*The British Invasion*
https://en.wikipedia.org/wiki/British_Invasion
https://www.rollingstone.com/music/music-news/the-british-invasion-from-the-beatles-to-the-stones-the-sixties-belonged-to-britain-244870/

*Novelty Songs*
https://www.waybackattack.com/top100-noveltyhits.html

*The Byrds*
https://en.wikipedia.org/wiki/The_Byrds
https://www.rollingstone.com/music/music-news/the-byrds-where-are-they-now-110074/

*"Louie Louie" by The Kingsmen*
https://www.marketplace.org/2018/04/23/history-song-louie-louie/

https://en.wikipedia.org/wiki/Louie_Louie

*Soul Train*
https://www.npr.org/2014/04/03/298736685/how-soul-train-shaped-a-generation
https://en.wikipedia.org/wiki/Soul_Train

*Shindig!*
https://en.wikipedia.org/wiki/Shindig!
https://www.metv.com/lists/shindig-shivaree-hullabaloo-and-the-great-rock-roll-shows-of-1965

The following trademarks and registered trademarks are the property of their respective holders: American Bandstand, The Animals, Batman, The Beatles, The Beach Boys, The Byrds, The Dave Clark Five, The Eagles, The Everly Brothers, The Hollies, Hullabaloo, Jan & Dean, The Kinks, MAD, Moog, Moog Synthesizer, Motown, Rickenbacker, The Righteous Brothers, The Rolling Stones, Shindig!, Song of the Century, Soul Train, The T.A.M.I. Show, Vox, The Who, Yamaha, The Yardbirds, Zildjian, The Zombies

# CHAPTER 11

# Revolution

The Baby Boomer generation was all about revolution, protest and social activism. In the late 60s and early 1970s, many Boomers actively participated in the following social movements: Anti-war, black power, civil rights, environmentalism, free speech, gay rights and women's liberation. Some Boomers were into counterculture, while others found the "Moral Majority" more to their way of thinking.

The Boomer era years of unrest and upheaval were unprecedented in American history. We witnessed the assassinations of John F. Kennedy, Medgar Evers, Martin Luther King, Malcolm X and Robert F. Kennedy... the civil rights demonstrations, marches and riots... the war in Vietnam and the anti-war movement... Kent State... the recreational use of drugs... the sexual revolution... a man walking on the moon... Watergate... and the resignation of Richard M. Nixon. Boomers lived through it all.

My experience was typical. I attended New York University, one of the centers of student unrest. I was the editor of a university satire magazine (fitting, don't you think?). I was #38 in the first military draft. Rather than go to Vietnam, which was a certainty in my case, I was fortunate enough to gain entry into the New York National Guard, where I was trained in riot suppression. Now *that's* poetic justice.

The various elements of revolution are so memorable that I have classified them as brands. Much as we consider rock 'n' roll songs and performers to be brands, we can think of the major personalities, events, places and symbols of the time as brands. Doing so helps us contextualize these decades of revolution and relate what happened then to popular culture.

Some examples: Martin Luther King was a strong person brand, the Vietnam War was a powerful event brand, Woodstock was a memorable place brand, and the "peace sign" was a highly motivational symbol brand.

As with rock 'n' roll, I have adjusted the Boomer era timeline in this chapter to go beyond the Boomer birth years. While younger Boomers may have been in their formative years during the protests of the late 60s and 1970s, many older Boomers may in fact have participated in these protests (or protested the protests). It is impossible not to acknowledge the influence that revolution had on the Boomer generation.

I hope you'll agree it is well worth broadening both the timeline and the definition of "brand" when you read about the "winners" and "losers" in this chapter.

## Jesse Jackson

Jesse Jackson helped pioneer the civil rights movement. In 1960, he participated at age nineteen in a sit-in at the Greenville, South Carolina public library. While in college, Jackson joined CORE (the Congress of Racial Equality) and became a supporter of Dr. Martin Luther King. Jackson walked with King in the famous Selma to Montgomery, Alabama march in 1965. A year later, he left his studies at the Chicago Theological Seminary to join King's Southern Christian Leadership Conference (SCLC). In 1967, he became national director of SCLC's business-focused "Operation Breadbasket." When King was gunned down in 1968, Jackson was by his side. A leadership struggle in the SCLC ensued. In 1971, Jackson left to form his own organization, "PUSH" (People United to Serve Humanity), which decades later was merged with Jackson's "Rainbow Coalition." Jackson sought the Democratic nomination for President in both 1984 and 1988. He has also been an international negotiator. Jesse Jackson is widely regarded as one of the most important civil rights figures of the 20th Century.

Photo credit: Jesse Jackson, 1983, *U.S. News and World Report* Collection, Library of Congress, public domain

## George Wallace

After George Wallace won the governorship of Alabama in 1962, he stated in his inaugural speech that he believed in "segregation now, segregation tomorrow, segregation forever." Wallace held true to those words, becoming nationally known for his bid in 1963 to stop two black students from enrolling at the University of Alabama. Wallace could not run for a second term as governor because of state law; his wife ran instead and won. He continued to preach racist policies even as he unsuccessfully ran for the presidency in 1964 and 1968 as an independent candidate, and in 1972 and 1976 as a Democratic candidate. Wallace was elected three more times as governor of Alabama. He was injured and left paralyzed in a 1972 assassination attempt. Later in his life, the segregationist tried his hand at doling out revisionist history, suggesting that his racist remarks were largely misunderstood. During his last term as governor, ending in 1986, he was credited with generally improving the state's economy. He died in 1998.

Photo credit: George C. Wallace at a news conference, some time between 1952 and 1986, *U.S. News and World Report* Collection, Library of Congress, public domain

## Robert F. Kennedy

Robert F. Kennedy, informally known as "Bobby," rose to national prominence as Attorney General in the administration of John F. Kennedy, his brother. As Attorney General, Kennedy was a fierce protector of civil rights, fought corruption in labor unions and went after organized crime. Not long after his brother was assassinated, Kennedy resigned as Attorney General, ran for a Senate seat in New York in 1964, and won. He became an outspoken critic of the war in Vietnam. A groundswell of support encouraged Kennedy to consider a presidential run, but he decided to enter the 1968 race only after he saw the primary success achieved by anti-war candidate Minnesota Senator Eugene McCarthy. When Martin Luther King was shot and killed, Kennedy made off-the-cuff comments that were widely praised for their consoling effect. Bobby Kennedy went on to win the California Democratic primary, but in June 1968, he was also assassinated, just two months after the death of Martin Luther King.

Photo credit: Robert F. Kennedy by Warren K. Leffler, Library of Congress, public domain

## 1968 Democratic National Convention

The August 1968 Democratic National Convention was destined for trouble. Sitting president Lyndon Johnson announced in March that he would not run and Robert F. Kennedy had been murdered in June. Vice President Hubert Humphrey quickly announced he would take Johnson's place, even as Senator Eugene McCarthy was lining up support for his anti-war candidacy. Meanwhile, thousands of protestors were flooding into Chicago, unhappy with any of the choices. Strong-arm mayor Richard Daley refused to issue permits to the protest organizers and vowed to squelch any uprisings. The convention became a publicly televised spectacle both inside and outside. Despite overwhelming support for anti-war candidates by primary voters, the "peace plank" was defeated, and Hubert Humphrey, who participated in none of the primaries, secured the nomination. "Yippie" protestors nominated a pig instead. Bloody riots took place on the streets. The crowd chanted, "The whole world is watching."

Photo credit: Scene across the street from the Hilton Hotel at Grant Park, Chicago, Democratic National Convention, August 26, 1968, *U.S. News and World Report* Collection, Library of Congress, public domain

## Peace Sign

The "peace sign" is a universally recognized, untrademarked symbol that is as strong as any brand the world has known. It was created by a British designer, Gerald Holtom, for the UK Campaign for Nuclear Disarmament (CND) in 1958. The symbol was always thought to be indicative of semaphore flag signals for the letters "N" and "D," superimposed one upon the other. While this appears to be accurate, Holtom wrote about his true inspiration: "I drew myself: the representative of an individual in despair, with hands palm outstretched outwards and downwards... I formalized the drawing into a line and put a circle round it." The symbol was first crafted into a crude button made from white clay and black paint, because the CND believed symbolically that a clay button could survive a nuclear blast. Later, the peace sign appeared on more traditional buttons and was adopted as the primary symbol of the American anti-war movement. Activists opposing nuclear power also used the peace sign in the 1980s. It remains an iconic symbol that is seen today in print, online, as jewelry and on clothing.

Photo credit: Raku peace sign ornament, Tony Alter, Flickr.com, CC BY 2.0

## Vietnam War

As early as 1950, America supported France in a French Indochina war that was being fought against communists. When France abandoned the effort in 1954, America stepped in and would remain embroiled until the war's unsuccessful end in 1973. As a revolutionary brand, "Vietnam" became one of the most divisive words, and wars, in American history. It revealed the horror of war because it was the first televised war. The war in Vietnam was pursued by presidents Kennedy, Johnson and Nixon. In 1962, 9,000 American troops were in South Vietnam. By mid-1965, there were 82,000 troops, and by late 1967, there were close to half a million, with deaths and casualties over 100,000. The war prompted some of the strongest protests the United States has ever seen, highlighted by attacks on college ROTC buildings, draft card burnings, young men exiting the U.S. for Canada, and massive anti-war demonstrations. The U.S. reached a peace agreement in 1973, but the war continued for two more years until North Vietnam defeated South Vietnam and united the country under communist rule.

Photo credit: Vietnam-The War Goes On, *LIFE* magazine, February 11, 1966, manhai, Flickr.com, CC BY 2.0

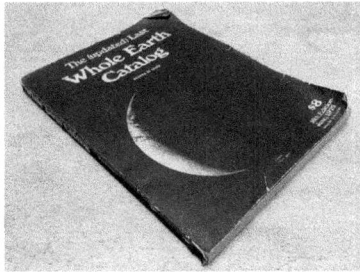

### Whole Earth Catalog

As much a counterculture brand as a product catalog, the "Whole Earth Catalog" was the brainchild of Stewart Brand, who wanted to revolutionize American society. First published in 1968, the Whole Earth Catalog celebrated individualism and a back-to-the-land philosophy. Brand included articles and commentary on self-sufficiency and ecology, but the publication was best known for its product descriptions of an eclectic assortment of "the best tools"; it encompassed literal tools as well as everything from books to educational courses. While descriptions and pictures were included, the Catalog merely listed contact information, so it was not truly a mail order catalog. The first edition of the Whole Earth Catalog was divided into these sections: Understanding Whole Systems, Shelter and Land Use, Industry and Craft, Communications, Community, Nomadics and Learning. From 1968 through 1972, the Catalog was published several times each year, and then only occasionally until 1998. It was highly influential in setting the tone for the counterculture movement.

Photo credit: Whole Earth Catalog, 1975, Akos Kokai, CC BY 2.0

## LSD

Strangely enough (and everything was strange when it came to LSD), the CIA was indirectly responsible for bringing LSD to the counterculture masses. Starting in the 50s, the CIA launched "Project MK-Ultra," in part to study mind control techniques for potential use in the Cold War. LSD was one of the hallucinogenic substances the CIA tested on volunteers and even unwitting subjects. A university student named Ken Kesey volunteered – yup, the same Ken Kesey who, with his "Merry Pranksters," spread the word far and wide in the early 60s that "acid" was cool. Harvard psychology professor Timothy Leary experimented with LSD on students at about the same time; he took it himself and was so blown away by the drug that he started a religion around it (the "League for Spiritual Discovery"), proclaiming to Boomers, "tune in, turn on, drop out." That's just what scores of hippies did. Some saw enlightenment while others experienced bad trips. LSD was the centerpiece brand of a 60s and 70s drug culture that popularized tripping and getting high to escape the world's problems.

Photo credit: Pixabay.com

## Ms. magazine

Ms. magazine had a very big aspiration: to translate the feminist movement into a magazine. In 1966, the National Organization for Women (NOW) was founded as the grassroots arm of the women's movement. This was one of the major events that spoke to the emergence of feminism. By 1971, a writer for *New York* magazine named Gloria Steinem became immersed in the feminist cause, co-founding both the Women's Action Alliance and the National Women's Political Caucus. Steinem, along with Letty Cottin Pogrebin, also began "Ms.," a magazine by and for women that was inserted as a sample into the December 1971 issue of *New York* magazine. Featuring such topics as "de-sexing" the English language and abortion, Ms. quickly became a feminist force. A first issue was officially published in July 1972. Within weeks, Ms. received 26,000 subscriptions and over 20,000 letters from readers. Ms. became the first national magazine brand to promote feminist journalism. Today, it continues to be at the forefront of addressing women's issues.

Photo credit: *Ms.*, Preview issue, Spring 1972, Ms. Magazine, CC BY-SA 4.0

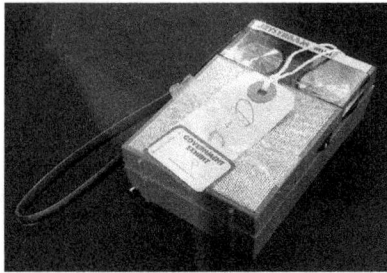

## Watergate

Watergate was such a renowned political brand that subsequent political and financial scandals frequently had "-gate" appended to them. In June 1972, burglars broke into Democratic National Committee headquarters, housed at the Watergate complex in Washington, DC. The break-in itself, which included stealing documents and wiretapping, paled in comparison to the furor that followed it. *Washington Post* reporters Bob Woodward and Carl Bernstein largely pieced together the details leading to the revelation, stunning at the time, that President Nixon's own Committee to Re-elect the President (wonderfully ridiculed as "CREEP") was behind the break-in. More significantly, Nixon, who at first maintained his innocence and was re-elected in 1972, was found to be involved in covering up the crime. By 1974, after the forced release of tapes that implicated the president, Nixon faced the prospect of being impeached. Instead, he resigned in August 1974. Watergate came to symbolize the abuse of political power and remains a black mark on the American presidency.

Photo credit: Transistor radio used in the Watergate break-in, Gerald R. Ford Presidential Museum, public domain

## Sources

*If you would like free access to a special webpage that includes all of the source links from this book, simply send your email address to: guidewordspub@gmail.com. In the subject line, type: WL Links. Your email will remain private and will not be shared or sold.*

*Revolution*
https://en.wikipedia.org/wiki/Counterculture_of_the_1960s

*Jesse Jackson*
https://www.history.com/topics/black-history/jesse-jackson
https://en.wikipedia.org/wiki/Jesse_Jackson

*George Wallace*
https://www.biography.com/political-figure/george-wallace
https://en.wikipedia.org/wiki/George_Wallace

*Robert F. Kennedy*
https://www.history.com/topics/1960s/robert-f-kennedy
https://en.wikipedia.org/wiki/Robert_F._Kennedy%27s_speech_on_the_assassination_of_Martin_Luther_King_Jr.

*1968 Democratic National Convention*
https://en.wikipedia.org/wiki/1968_Democratic_National_Convention
https://www.history.com/topics/1960s/1968-democratic-convention

*Peace sign*
https://www.fastcompany.com/3036540/the-untold-story-of-the-peace-sign
https://en.wikipedia.org/wiki/Peace_symbols

*Vietnam War*
https://www.history.com/topics/vietnam-war/vietnam-war-history

*Whole Earth Catalog*
https://en.wikipedia.org/wiki/Whole_Earth_Catalog
http://www.wholeearth.com/history-whole-earth-catalog.php

*LSD*
https://www.history.com/topics/crime/history-of-lsd

*Ms. magazine*
https://msmagazine.com/about/
http://nymag.com/news/features/ms-magazine-2011-11/

*Watergate*
https://www.history.com/topics/1970s/watergate

The following trademarks and registered trademarks are the property of their respective holders: Campaign for Nuclear Disarmament, CORE, LIFE, Moral Majority, Ms., New York University, NOW, Rainbow Coalition, SCLC, Whole Earth Catalog, Woodstock, Yippie

# Environment

Rachel Carson's book, *Silent Spring*, published in the early 60s, became the springboard for the environmental movement. The book called attention to the damaging effects of the pesticide DDT, just as Ralph Nader's 1964 book, *Unsafe at Any Speed*, chided automobile makers for polluting the air.

Both of these books helped raise the country's environmental consciousness. Boomers quickly adopted environmentalism as one of their causes, demonstrating on behalf of a cleaner, safer planet. Protecting "Mother Earth" became as compelling a cause as social justice, made even more urgent by such events as the 1969 Santa Barbara, California oil spill and the 1979 Three Mile Island nuclear reactor accident. It may surprise you to learn that the first mention of "climate change" was in a 1956 study, "The Carbon Dioxide Theory of Climatic Change," by Gilbert Plass, a physicist. The concept of "global warming" first appeared in a 1975 paper by Wallace Broecker, a geochemist at Columbia University.

There were no "green brands" to speak of in the 60s; it wasn't until the 1970s that true eco-friendly brands such as Patagonia and Tom's of Maine began to gain traction. The earliest green brands highlighted the idea of "back to nature" and featured pure, natural and often organic ingredients. Only in later years were green brands increasingly common.

Instead, the environmental brands of the 50s, 60s and early 70s were primarily not-for-profit organizations, such as The Nature Conservancy (1951), Keep America Beautiful (1953), the World Wildlife Fund (1961), the Environmental Defense Fund (1967), Friends of the Earth (1969), Greenpeace (1971) and the Cousteau Society (1973). One might also think of "Earth Day" (initiated on April 22, 1970) as well as the "EPA" (the Environmental Protection Agency, formed in 1970) as environmental brands of a sort.

While Boomer era environmentalism resulted in a flurry of state and federal regulations designed to protect the environment, environmental disasters such as oil spills, toxic water supplies and nuclear reactor meltdowns would continue to plague America and the world in later decades. In addition, the global impact of "climate change" would become one of the most serious issues of our time.

## The Nature Conservancy

The Nature Conservancy, originally called the Ecologists Union, was founded in 1951 in Washington, DC, long before the environmental movement even began. Renowned for land preservation, this not-for-profit organization takes a scientific approach to conservation. It began purchasing land in the United States to protect it as early as 1961. In recent years, The Nature Conservancy has broadened its priorities to include addressing climate change, protecting land and water, providing food and water sustainably, and building healthy cities. While it started in the United States, The Nature Conservancy today impacts conservation in 72 countries. The organization has more than 400 scientists and more than one million members. It has protected over 119 million acres of land and operates more than 100 marine conservation projects. A non-partisan organization, The Nature Conservancy believes in working collaboratively with landowners, businesses and government agencies in an effort to show how nature can provide effective solutions to major challenges like climate change.

Photo credit: Hardwoods and white pines at West Branch Forest Preserve, a Nature Conservancy preserve, Nicholas A. Tonelli, Flickr.com, CC BY 2.0

## Big Oil

Oil companies are distinct brands, but beginning in the late 60s, the largest public oil companies were grouped together and branded "Big Oil." This term specifically applies to the world's largest non-state oil companies, sometimes referred to as "supermajors." Over the years, the nickname has also been used to represent the oil and gas industry as a whole in a negative manner, suggesting its broad and powerful influence. The companies that originally made up the supermajors were BP, Chevron, Conoco Phillips, Exxon Mobil, Royal Dutch Shell, Total and Eni. Big Oil is something of a misnomer as it relates to the influence of these companies today. In fact, the fourteen nations of OPEC (Organization of the Petroleum Exporting Companies) are more important in setting global oil prices. Now the Big Oil companies are involved in a significant effort to rebrand themselves as being climate-conscious, touting a new emphasis on less fossil fuel and more "green" forms of energy. Some people think that's a lot of hot air.

Photo credit: Oil drums, Bradley Gordon, Flickr.com, CC BY 2.0

## Environmental Defense Fund

After Rachel Carson's *Silent Spring* put the dangers of DDT into the national spotlight, a small conservation group was documenting the decline of the osprey on Long Island, New York. Significant concentrations of DDT were discovered in unhatched osprey eggs, so the group asked the local county to stop using the pesticide for mosquito control. When the county refused, the group got themselves an attorney and went to court on behalf of the environment, highly unusual at the time. The result was a local ban on DDT in 1966, followed by a statewide ban. In 1972, the use of DDT was forbidden nationally. The group that started it all launched the not-for-profit Environmental Defense Fund (EDF) in 1967. By the 1990s, EDF was fostering corporate partnerships and gaining international prominence. Today, the EDF focuses on climate (clean energy), the oceans (sustainable fishing), ecosystems (food, water and shelter) and health (reducing exposure to pollutants). The EDF is more than two million members strong and has become a superbrand in the environmental arena.

Photo credit: Osprey on Seedskadee National Wildlife Refuge, USFWS Mountain-Prairie, Flickr.com, CC BY 2.0

## Smog

The Environmental Defense Fund reports that nearly 40 percent of Americans live in areas with unhealthy levels of smog pollution. The word "smog," a combination of smoke and fog, originated in the early 20<sup>th</sup> Century, referring to the thick hazy pollution caused largely by industrial emissions. The popularity of the automobile contributed to the problem. Today, "smog" is a brand of sorts – a universally recognized environmental malady. It is caused by a wide variety of emissions, including industry, coal, combustion, vehicles, and forest fires. It becomes even more apparent during an inversion, when warmer air is held above cooler air. This forces pollution closer to the ground so it becomes all the more dangerous to humans and animals. You may have seen news reports of afflicted areas in which the smog is so severe that cities are shrouded in it and people are wearing masks. Smog is toxic and can cause respiratory illnesses, a shortened life span and even premature death.

Photo credit: Smog, Santiago, Chile, Eduardo Zarate, Flickr.com, CC BY-ND 2.0

### Earth Day

"Earth Day" was inspired by the student anti-war movement and precipitated by the 1969 Santa Barbara, California oil spill. Taking a cue from the student activists, Democratic Senator Gaylord Nelson conceived Earth Day as an environmental "national teach-in," teaming up with Republican Congressman Pete McCloskey. April 22 was selected to encourage college students to be involved; the date fell between Spring break and final exams. On April 22, 1970, some twenty million Americans joined in coast-to-coast demonstrations while thousands of colleges and universities launched anti-pollution protests. Disparate environmental groups came together in a common cause. Earth Day directly influenced the creation of the Environmental Protection Agency and the passage of the Clean Air, Clean Water and Endangered Species Acts, all in 1970. Twenty years later Earth Day 1990 became a global event, with 200 million people in 141 countries involved. Earth Day continues annually as the largest secular observance in the world.

Photo credit: Blue Marble-2002, NASA Goddard Space Flight Center, Flickr.com, CC BY 2.0

## Coal

"Coal" has been an energy source for thousands of years, and it continues to be relied on today. In the United States, coal was used as early as the 1740s. It became the dominant source of energy in the late 1800s and early 1900s. By the 1940s, it was providing more than half of the country's energy. It was only in the 50s that the use of petroleum for energy exceeded the use of coal. In the 60s, large companies, including oil companies and producers of electricity, began to acquire producers of coal. The 1973 oil crisis spiked coal prices, but they declined in the 1980s because the worldwide supply was plentiful. In recent years, the coal "brand" has come under fire because of its negative effect on the environment. According to the Union of Concerned Scientists, "The same chemistry that enables coal to produce energy – the breaking down of carbon molecules – also produces a number of profoundly harmful environmental impacts and pollutants that harm public health." Despite this, some coal-producing states are hesitant to move away from it because of the economic consequences.

Photo credit: New torch, coal mine, b3tarev3, Flickr.com, public domain

## Greenpeace

In 1971, a small group of concerned activists sailed in a small fishing boat from Vancouver, Canada to Alaska's Amchitka Island. They were protesting U.S. nuclear testing off the coast of Alaska and decided the only way to get attention was to endanger themselves by their physical presence. The U.S. Coast Guard intervened, but the group made headlines because of their peaceful protest. That was the birth of Greenpeace. Today Greenpeace is one of the most recognized environmental brands, with 250,000 U.S. members and 2.8 million members worldwide who provide its funding. Greenpeace does not solicit contributions from governments or businesses, nor does it endorse political candidates. The direct actions of Greenpeace have sometimes sparked controversy and crossed legal lines, but the organization has been highly successful in raising public awareness of serious environmental issues. Greenpeace has been credited with helping to ban commercial whaling, protect Antarctica and stop nuclear testing.

Photo credit: Greenpeace at Latitude 2010, Howard Lake, Flickr.com, CC BY-SA 2.0

## Three Mile Island

On March 28, 1979, the Unit 2 reactor at Three Mile Island near Middletown, Pennsylvania partially melted down. According to the U.S. Nuclear Regulatory Commission (NRC), the nuclear power plant experienced a failure in the secondary, non-nuclear section of the plant. A series of mishaps caused the reactor coolant pumps to stop circulating water, which resulted in the core overheating. While the reactor was seriously damaged, the health effects of leaked radiation were minimal. The NRC reported that "the actual release had negligible effects on the physical health of individuals or the environment." Still, "Three Mile Island," which was officially closed in 2019, came to be associated with the meltdown risk of a nuclear power plant. The accident led to major changes in the nuclear power industry and the way in which the NRC oversees nuclear power plants. The accident also contributed to a reduction in the use of nuclear power in the U.S. The Three Mile Island incident was overshadowed by two more recent nuclear disasters: Chernobyl (1986) and Fukuchima Daiichi (2011).

Photo credit: Environmental Protection Agency, public domain

## Patagonia

Founded in 1973 in Ventura, California by accomplished rock climber Yvon Chouinard, Patagonia is a clothing company with a reputation for environmental activism. Patagonia, Inc. was an outgrowth of climbing gear company Chouinard Equipment, which filed for bankruptcy in 1989. The company's soft goods division, which sold clothing, was retained by Yvon Chouinard under the brand name "Patagonia." Since its beginning, the company has supported grassroots environmental activists and today gives 1 percent of its sales to support environmental organizations around the world. Patagonia gives grants of up to $15,000 to hundreds of groups every year; grants awarded in 2018 exceeded $100 million. The company also participates in a broad range of environmental and social initiatives, including a recent campaign to save public lands and water in the United States from development. Patagonia is a "B Corp," a type of corporation that meets "the highest standards of verified social and environmental performance, public transparency and legal accountability to balance profit and purpose."

Photo credit: Patagonia Label-1, Ajay Suresh, Flickr.com, CC BY 2.0

## Plastics

In the 1967 film, *The Graduate*, young Ben Braddock (Dustin Hoffman) receives this friendly advice from an adult at a party: "Plastics. ... There's a great future in plastics." That may have been when "plastics" became a noteworthy "brand" of the 60s, but environmental concerns over plastic have reached a feverish pitch today. Its impact on the environment, particularly oceans, has been nefarious. *National Geographic* has started to track anti-plastic initiatives, and the list paints a fascinating picture of a budding environmental movement. Here are just a few examples: In July 2018, Seattle became the first U.S. city to ban plastic straws and utensils, and Disney announced a ban on single-use plastic straw and stirrers at all of its theme parks and resorts. In September 2018, California implemented a state-wide partial ban on plastic straws. In October 2018, the European Parliament approved a measure to significantly reduce single-use plastic across Europe. In January 2019, San Diego banned Styrofoam food and drink containers. In June 2019, Canada said it would ban single-use plastics by 2021.

Photo credit: Plastic cups, English Wikipedia user Daniel Case, CC BY-SA 3.0

## Sources

*If you would like free access to a special webpage that includes all of the source links from this book, simply send your email address to: guidewordspub@gmail.com. In the subject line, type: WL Links. Your email will remain private and will not be shared or sold.*

*Environment*
https://skepticalscience.com/climate-change-global-warming-basic.html
https://adage.com/article/adage-encyclopedia/environmental-movement/98455

*The Nature Conservancy*
https://www.nature.org/en-us/

*Big Oil*
https://en.wikipedia.org/wiki/Big_Oil
https://grist.org/article/the-billion-dollar-rebrand-how-big-oil-is-trying-to-change-its-image/

*Environmental Defense Fund*
https://www.edf.org/about/our-history

*Smog*
https://www.edf.org/health/why-smog-standards-are-important-our-health
https://en.wikipedia.org/wiki/Smog

*Earth Day*
https://www.earthday.org/about/the-history-of-earth-day/?

*Coal*
https://en.wikipedia.org/wiki/History_of_coal_mining_in_the_United_States
https://www.ucsusa.org/clean-energy/coal-and-other-fossil-fuels/coal-air-pollution

*Greenpeace*
https://www.greenpeace.org/usa/about/

https://en.wikipedia.org/wiki/Greenpeace

*Three Mile Island*
https://www.nrc.gov/reading-rm/doc-collections/fact-sheets/3mile-isle.html
https://en.wikipedia.org/wiki/Three_Mile_Island_accident

*Patagonia*
https://www.patagonia.com/environmental-grants-and-support.html
https://en.wikipedia.org/wiki/Patagonia_(clothing)
https://bcorporation.net/about-b-corps

*Plastics*
https://en.wikipedia.org/wiki/Plastic
https://www.nationalgeographic.com/environment/2018/07/ocean-plastic-pollution-solutions/

The following trademarks and registered trademarks are the property of their respective holders: BP, Chevron, Columbia University, Conoco Phillips, Cousteau Society, Earth Day, Eni, Environmental Defense Fund, Exxon Mobil, Friends of the Earth, Greenpeace, Keep America Beautiful, Patagonia, Royal Dutch Shell, Styrofoam, The Nature Conservancy, Tom's of Maine, Total, Union of Concerned Scientists

# Technology

When we think of "technology," it is likely to be in the context of information technology, biotechnology, or perhaps environmental technology. None of those technologies existed in any meaningful form in the 50s and 60s.

But technology was very much a part of the lives of Boomer kids – it was just different kinds of technology. The most enticing technological advancement was television (and eventually color television). However, there were other thrilling innovations, such as the 45 rpm records that created a market for "single" hits, and transistor radios, which made it possible for kids to carry around radio stations that played their favorite rock 'n' roll tunes.

Other technologies would become important to the lives of Boomer kids. For example, the push button ("Touch-Tone") telephone replaced the rotary dial in 1963, heralding a new era of easier teen talk. The Polaroid Land camera amazed Boomer kids by producing instantly developed photographs. The microwave helped mom create almost-instant meals.

Magnetic tape came into its own, affecting Boomers in two ways: On the video side, television shows could be recorded on tape instead of film; by 1963, "instant replay" became a feature of sports events. On the audio side, the 8-track tape made it possible for teens to play their favorite albums in their cars (even if the tape jammed every now and then). That was followed by the equally unreliable cassette tape.

Technology was changing in the world around Boomer kids as well. In 1959, the first commercial plain paper copier introduced by Xerox revolutionized the duplication process. Also in 1959, two patents were granted for tiny electronic circuits known as "microchips," the core of just about every technology device we use today. Jet airliners began to fly domestically and internationally in the 50s. The 1957 launch of the first U.S. satellite ended in failure, but it would foreshadow future space successes, including astronauts landing on the moon in 1969.

Commercial computers appeared in the 50s, but the first personal computer did not come along until 1975 – and even then, it was in the form of a kit. The early 60s saw the introduction of the IBM Selectric typewriter, the invention of the laser, and the first use of a factory robot. The first computer mouse was invented in 1964 and the earliest version of video games appeared in 1966.

The Boomer era brought with it technological changes of great significance, even if the Information Age was still in its infancy.

### 45 rpm Record

RCA Victor issued the first 7-inch 45 rpm (revolutions per minute) vinyl record in 1949, about nine months after Columbia produced the first 33-1/3 rpm LP (Long Playing) record. Both of these formats were enthusiastically embraced by Boomer kids. Early on, monaural "45s" reigned supreme since they carried the single hits that typified the rock 'n' roll era. Performing artists and their songs became known, but young music aficionados also began to recognize such record label brands as Decca, Reprise, Sun and most notably, Motown – renowned for the "Motown sound." Pop charts were based on the sales of single hits. Radio disc jockeys would "spin discs" and the TV show "American Bandstand" would feature lip-syncing stars crooning while kids danced in the studio. Boomer kids in their later teens and early twenties found stereo LPs more to their liking. The emergence of British rock and psychedelic or acid rock created a market for longer songs and thematic albums, often encased in elaborate artistic album covers.

Photo credit: Elvis Presley, "Hound Dog," SUN Records 45 rpm, JFHayeur, Flickr.com, CC BY-SA 2.0

## 8-Track Tape

You can thank the 50s and 60s car culture for the development of the 8-track tape. Earl Muntz created the "Stereo-Pak" four-track stereo cartridge system for automobiles in 1962. The Lear Jet Corporation invented the "Stereo 8" tape cartridge for RCA in 1964. Ford Motor Company liked it so much that eight-track tape players were offered as an installed option in 1966 Mustangs, Lincolns and Thunderbirds. The next model year, Ford offered this option on all of its cars. Teens of the time loved having their favorite albums available to play in their cars, so it wasn't long before this technology was introduced into homes. Eight-track tapes were convenient and portable, easily moving back and forth from car to home. Some consumers even saw them as a replacement for LPs. By the late 60s, eight-track tapes were so popular that record companies produced tape versions of their vinyl records within a month of release. However, with the advent of the smaller, portable cassette tape in 1962, the eight-track tape declined in popularity and virtually disappeared by the early 1980s.

Photo credit: 8-track tape, Erkaha, CC BY-SA 4.0

### Transistor Radio

The invention of the transistor in 1947 created a market for smaller, portable radios – just in time for the rock 'n' roll era. The first transistor radio to hit the market in 1954 was the result of a two-company effort: Texas Instruments designed it and the Regency Division of I.D.E.A. manufactured it. Named the "Regency TR-1," almost 100,000 units of the radio were sold in the first year despite the radio's mediocre quality. Raytheon produced a better transistor radio in 1955, and that opened the floodgates for other major manufacturers to enter the market, including Crosley, DeWald, RCA, Sony and Zenith. Unlike the eight-track tape that was originally designed for automobiles, the transistor radio was a portable product Boomer kids could carry with them. But it also appeared in cars: Chrysler and Philco introduced the first all-transistor car radio in 1955. By the 1970s, billions of transistor radios had been manufactured. They remained the most popular form of portable entertainment until the 1980s, when they were replaced by CD players and then personal audio players.

Photo credit: Philco transistor radio, circa 1958, Joe Haupt, Flickr.com, CC BY 2.0

## de Havilland DH 106 Comet Jetliner

Jet air travel was a luxury for most Boomer kids, but during the Boomer era, the jetliner was coming into its own, with Pan Am and TWA pioneering transatlantic travel. Commercial air travel had some big hurdles to overcome, though. The DH 106 Comet, built by de Havilland and introduced in 1952, was the world's first commercial jet airliner. The Comet paved the way for passenger air travel, but it also gained a reputation for unreliability. Not long after its introduction, three Comets perished in accidents within twelve months. The problems of the Comet actually allowed competitive airplane manufacturers like Boeing and Douglas to learn from de Havilland's mistakes and produce safer jets. The Comet was completely redesigned and went through model revisions. The Comet 4 series, introduced in 1958, was used by the British airline BOAC and remained in circulation for at least thirty years. Still, the Comet would never achieve the success of other jet planes. In aviation history, the Comet has likely become known more for the improvement of accident investigations than anything else.

Photo credit: de Havilland DH 106 Comet, RuthAS, CC BY 3.0

## Polaroid Land Camera

One of the more ingenious and remarkable inventions of the Boomer era was instant photography. Scientist Edwin Land first developed self-developing film in the 1940s and founded Polaroid Corporation. The "Polaroid Land Camera Model 95," introduced in late 1948, was the first camera to produce instant sepia-colored photographic prints in about one minute. The original process, which involved peeling apart a negative and a print, was dramatically improved over time, as was the quality of the output. In 1963, Polaroid introduced "Polacolor," the first instant color film. It wasn't until 1972 that the "Polaroid SX-70" camera (Land's name was dropped after he retired from the company) produced the instant photograph format for which Polaroid is best known: a fully formed color print in a plastic white frame. Boomer kids couldn't get enough of instant photography – it appeased their need for instant gratification. But Polaroid wasn't just a hit with consumers – photographers and artists, most famously Andy Warhol, made extensive use of instant photography technology.

Photo credit: Polaroid Automatic 104, 1965-67, Terri Monahan, Flickr.com, CC BY-SA 2.0

## Kodak Instamatic Camera

Make no mistake about it – the "Kodak Instamatic" camera, first introduced in 1963, was a major brand success story. On that basis, I hesitate to label it a "loser," so I'd better explain my rationale. Kodak was already a leading maker of film in the 50s and 60s. Just like razor companies that wanted to sell more blades, Kodak wanted to sell more film. By creating the Instamatic, they could do just that: This very inexpensive point-and-shoot camera encouraged *everyone*, even Boomer kids, to become amateur photographers. Kodak effectively created a whole new market for photography, separate from professional photographers who tended to use more expensive, high quality cameras made by European and Japanese companies. The more pictures people took with an Instamatic, the more film they used. It didn't matter if the photographs were lousy, it was film consumption that mattered. In fact, the Instamatic became a cash cow for Kodak's film business. The bottom line: Instamatics weren't about taking quality photographs, they were about selling film; hence, my "loser" designation.

Photo credit: Kodak 6/365 Instamatic camera, Ryan Hyde, Flickr.com, CC BY-SA 2.0

### Xerox 914 Copier

We take making copies for granted today, but in the 50s, modern copying didn't yet exist. A photographic paper and equipment manufacturer, The Haloid Photographic Company, developed a process they named "xerography," derived from the Greek words for "dry writing." In 1959, the company, which had changed its name to Haloid Xerox, introduced the "Xerox 914" copier. It used a dry toner process to copy onto plain paper, a first. An ad campaign featured monkeys making copies by simply touching a button. The product was such an astounding success that the company renamed itself Xerox Corporation and recorded close to $60 million in sales by the end of 1961. In 1963, Xerox introduced the first desktop plain paper copier, and the company remained the leading copier manufacturer throughout the 60s. Probably its most famous ad campaign was launched in the 1970s, when a monk named "Brother Dominic" used a Xerox copier instead of making illuminated copies by hand. Despite its trademarked name, "Xerox" has entered our lexicon as a word that universally represents "copy."

Photo credit: Xerox 914 copier, Museum of Business History and Technology in Delaware, Marcin Wichary, CC BY 2.0

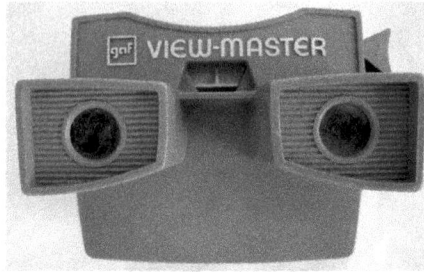

### View-Master

Debuting in 1939, the "View-Master" was a stereoscope device that used cardboard reels with pairs of photographic images that appeared to be three-dimensional when viewed. It became popular with Boomer kids in the 50s after View-Master acquired a competitor and gained licensing rights to Walt Disney Studios. Throughout the 50s and 60s, newer, more streamlined versions of the View-Master were introduced, including the first plastic model in 1962, along with an ever-increasing line of reels. When GAF bought the company in 1966, the reels appealed to Boomer kids by relying on tie-ins with cartoon characters and television shows. However, the decades-old technology was aging; it could never really compete with color television and the movies. GAF tried to keep View-Master vibrant by introducing "talking" models and projectors in the 1970s and 1980s. In an effort to maintain brand relevance, Mattel, the current owner of View-Master, teamed with Google to produce a "View-Master Virtual Reality Viewer." A movie based on View-Master is also being considered. Really?!

Photo credit: View-Master, Deiby Chico, Flickr.com, CC BY 2.0

## Touch-Tone Telephone

Boomer kids (and their moms) sure liked talking on the telephone. Not to be sexist, but it was largely adolescent and teenage girls who burned up the telephone lines, spending hours chatting with their friends. A prized birthday gift for a Boomer kid was getting his or her own phone (a land line phone with a physical cord was the only option back then). Of course, conversations with a boyfriend or girlfriend often had to be conducted in the privacy of a closet! Telephone technology kept up with our communication needs. In 1959, the Bell System's "Princess," brilliantly targeting women, featured a low-profile design, a light-up dial that functioned as a night light, and a remarkable range of colors. It was the perfect accessory for any bedroom. In 1963, a revolutionary technology known as "dual-tone multi-frequency" was introduced by Bell under the name, "Touch-Tone." How exciting it was to push those buttons and here the different tones! It took twenty years for Touch-Tone technology to replace rotary or pulse dialing, but push-button phones eventually became a worldwide standard.

Photo credit: Touch-Tone keypad, Bill Bradford, Flickr.com, CC BY 2.0

## First U.S. Satellite Launch

As children of the Space Age, Boomer kids fell in love with U.S. astronauts, rocket ships and space travel. Space permeated popular culture via TV shows, cartoons, movies, comic books, toys and even such foods as "Space Food Sticks" and "Tang." Americans were dismayed when the U.S.S.R. successfully launched Sputnik, the world's first artificial satellite, in October 1957. Sputnik 2, carrying Laika the dog, followed in November. Not to be outdone, the U.S. accelerated its own satellite launch program. Perhaps prematurely, it rushed to launch the Vanguard rocket, which carried a small satellite, on December 6, 1957. The rocket got four feet off the ground and exploded. Remarkably, the satellite was ejected from the nose of the rocket unscathed, but the blown launch inspired the skeptical American press to call it "Kaputnik" or "Flopnik." Subsequent launches succeeded, and the U.S. learned from its mistakes. In 1961, Alan Shepard became the first U.S. astronaut to orbit the Earth, and in 1969, NASA's Apollo 11 mission successfully put Neil Armstrong and Buzz Aldrin on the moon.

Photo credit: Vanguard rocket explodes, Dec. 6, 1957, public domain

## Sources
*If you would like free access to a special webpage that includes all of the source links from this book, simply send your email address to: guidewordspub@gmail.com. In the subject line, type: WL Links. Your email will remain private and will not be shared or sold.*

*45 rpm Records*
https://en.wikipedia.org/wiki/Single_(music)

*8-track Tape*
https://en.wikipedia.org/wiki/8-track_tape

*Transistor Radio*
https://en.wikipedia.org/wiki/Transistor_radio

*de Havilland DH 106 Comet Jetliner*
https://en.wikipedia.org/wiki/De_Havilland_Comet

*Polaroid Land Camera*
https://en.wikipedia.org/wiki/Land_Camera
https://garage.vice.com/en_us/article/wj48y4/andy-warhols-polaroids-are-his-most-influential-works

*Kodak Instamatic Camera*
https://en.wikipedia.org/wiki/Instamatic

*Xerox 914 Copier*
https://en.wikipedia.org/wiki/Xerox

*View-Master*
https://en.wikipedia.org/wiki/View-Master

*Touch-Tone Telephone*
https://en.wikipedia.org/wiki/Princess_telephone
https://en.wikipedia.org/wiki/Push-button_telephone

*First U.S. Space Launch*
https://www.nasa.gov/feature/60-years-ago-vanguard-fails-to-reach-orbit
https://en.wikipedia.org/wiki/Apollo_11

The following trademarks and registered trademarks are the property of their respective holders: Bell System, BOAC, Boeing, Chrysler, Columbia, Comet, Crosley, de Havilland, Decca, DeWald, Douglas, Ford, GAF, Google, IBM, Instamatic, Kodak, Lear Jet, Lincoln, Mattel, Motown, Mustang, NASA, Pan Am, Philco, Polacolor, Polaroid, Princess, RCA, RCA Victor, Regency, Reprise, Selectric, Sony, Stereo 8, Stereo-Pak, SUN, SX-70, Texas Instruments, Thunderbird, Touch-Tone, TWA, View-Master, Xerox, Zenith

# CHAPTER 14

# Movies

Movies had a big influence on Boomer kids in the 50s and 60s. The new medium, television, was ascending. There was no Internet, no streaming, no smartphones, no tablets, no personal computers. Second only to TV (and perhaps comic books), the "big screen" filled a need for escapism.

Going to the movies was a real entertainment experience, especially those Saturday matinees. Maybe your mom or dad would drop you and a sibling and friend off so you could feel like an adult going to the movies by yourself. The price of a ticket was cheap. The movie theatre was elaborately adorned inside, with a gold inlaid ceiling, big red curtains, and plush seats. You would buy popcorn, candy and a soda. You'd see a double feature, and there was a short cartoon too. You could spend the whole afternoon there. The mean old ushers would shine their flashlights and tell all the kids to keep quiet and stop throwing stuff. But of course, *you* were well-behaved, right?

When you were older, you would go to the movie theatre in the evening on a date with a boy or girl you liked. There would be a pretty good chance that you wouldn't even be watching the whole movie. I'm sure you know what I mean!

Movie studios had to aggressively compete with television back then, so they tried various ways to differentiate film from the small screen. Movie screens got bigger to accommodate "CinemaScope" and color got bolder thanks to "Technicolor." Some longer movies even had intermissions. Novel add-ons such as "3-D" (for which you needed red and blue glasses) and "Smell-O-Vision" were tried, but most of them failed.

Movies were classified into a variety of genres. There were plenty of animated and family films that targeted Boomer kids, along with quirky genres, such as horror and science fiction and later, beach party and spy movies.

When you think about the construct of a movie, you begin to see that it really is a perfect example of branding. In the 50s and 60s, each movie had its own title, often executed in a distinguishing typeface. Each movie had its own graphic look and image, which was a key part of a movie poster, a magazine ad, and maybe a billboard. Trailers for TV proliferated. Each movie had its own theme song. And, of course, each movie featured a specific plot and characters played by Hollywood stars. A movie was a tidy, self-contained brand package.

With the hundreds of movies produced in the 50s and 60s, it is impossible to hone down the list to a handful, so I've limited my "winners" and "losers" to movies that represent some of the genres that appealed directly to Boomer kids. I suspect my picks may spark a controversy or two!

## Lady and the Tramp (Animation)

The 1955 animated film, *Lady and the Tramp*, is a prime example of the increasing sophistication of full-length animated movies. The first animated movie filmed in CinemaScope, it told the story of the very proper "Lady," an upper-class cocker spaniel, and "Tramp," a street-wise mutt who falls in love with her. Despite a lukewarm reception from some critics of the day, *Lady and the Tramp* grossed more than any other Disney animated feature since the 1937 film, *Snow White and the Seven Dwarfs*. This was just one of scores of animated feature films made by Walt Disney in the 50s and 60s. Disney dominated animated films at the time, sometimes releasing several in a single year. Among the animated classics produced by the film studio arm of Disney were *Cinderella* (1950), *Alice in Wonderland* (1951), *Peter Pan* (1953), *Sleeping Beauty* (1959), *One Hundred and One Dalmatians* (1961), *The Sword in the Stone* (1963) and *The Jungle Book* (1967). A substantial number of Disney animated films, as well as live action and documentary films, focused on animals.

Photo credit: Lady and the Tramp vintage Valentine, Karen Horton, Flickr.com, CC BY 2.0

### Hey There, It's Yogi Bear! (Animation)

It's hard to debate the good-natured fun of the "Yogi Bear" character and his jovial attitude toward authority. He also surrounded himself with lovable characters, such as "BooBoo" and "Cindy Bear." So why does this 1964 animated feature film from Hanna-Barbera get a "thumbs down"? Basically, because the movie was a longer version of the animated children's television program, "The Yogi Bear Show." It is a classic attempt to capitalize on a successful TV program by producing a movie. As this film and other animated feature films in the 50s and 60s proved, transitioning from a television cartoon show to the big screen can be problematic. *Hey There, It's Yogi Bear!* simply doesn't have the engaging story, action and adventure, musical score or animation finesse of arch-rival Disney – certainly not enough to qualify as a feature film. Of course, very few studios could compete with Disney... so maybe we should just leave it at that. Unless an animated movie in the 50s and 60s had the Disney name on it, it probably was not a first-rate production.

Photo credit: Yogi Bear cartoon cards game, Mark Anderson, Flickr.com, CC BY 2.0

### Creature from the Black Lagoon (Horror)

The 50s prompted a raft of horror movies, most of them low budget. The country was moving on from World War II, but it was still a presence in America's rear-view mirror. The Cold War was heating up and nuclear disaster was a real threat. The catastrophic consequences of war and the fear of another conflict combined to create an atmosphere that was ripe for horror and its sister genre, science fiction. Many horror movies featured monsters that wreaked havoc on contemporary towns and cities. Audiences, in particular kids, were terrorized by the evil unleashed by these creatures, but nervous laughter was a common reaction too, especially when monsters were strangely attracted to beautiful women. *The Creature from the Black Lagoon* was a 1954 horror flick shown in big cities in 3D and simple black-and-white in other cities. "Gill-man" rises from an Amazon lagoon, killing humans but falling for the hero's fiancée. The scary tale was such a hit it led to two sequels. Today this film is considered a classic of the horror genre.

Photo credit: Movie poster, Creature from the Black Lagoon, copyright 1954, Universal Pictures Co., Inc., public domain

## House on Haunted Hill (Horror)

Boomer kids seemed to adore a kind of horror film that focused on the macabre. The master of the genre was the filmmaker William Castle, who created a slew of B movies in the 50s and 60s. *House on Haunted Hill* (1959) featured the horror movie actor, Vincent Price, as a demented millionaire who offers money to unsuspecting victims if they agree to spend the night in his haunted house. Every Castle film had a gimmick. In *House on Haunted Hill*, it was "Emergo," a plastic skeleton that was installed in movie theatres and floated over the audience. For the movie *The Tingler* (1959), "Percepto" vibrators were attached to some movie theatre seats. The 1960 film *13 Ghosts* had "Illusion-O" so audience members could use a viewer to make ghosts appear or disappear. Castle's movies were completely absurd, but they were frightening. Kids loved them and they made money. Castle is said to have influenced another filmmaker of scary movies by the name of Alfred Hitchcock.

Photo credit: Movie poster, House on Haunted Hill, copyright 1958, Allied Artists, public domain

### The Day the Earth Stood Still (Science Fiction)

Science fiction, especially as it related to outer space, was a wildly popular subject during the 50s and 60s, as evidenced in television shows, comic books and movies. Even the "Superman" character was born on the planet Krypton. *The Day the Earth Stood Still* was a 1951 science fiction movie that was timely for two reasons: It took advantage of contemporary interest in flying saucers, and it conveyed a message of peace to humanity. Directed by Robert Wise and starring a cast of well-known actors (unusual for a science fiction film), *The Day the Earth Stood Still* was one of the early "alien visits Earth" movies. In this case, a humanoid alien, Klaatu, and his robot, Gort, come to our planet. The humans are unwelcoming, but some of them befriend Klaatu. The message of the film is clear when Klaatu announces he was sent by an interplanetary organization to warn humans not to pursue wars. There have been claims that the movie is a metaphor for Christ's second coming. While it was only modestly successful upon release, in later years, this film has been praised for the urgency of its anti-war plea.

Photo credit: Movie poster, The Day the Earth Stood Still, Peabody Essex Museum, the Kirk Hammett Collection, Larry Lamsa, Flickr.com, CC BY 2.0

### The Blob (Science Fiction)

In the 1958 science fiction film, *The Blob*, the alien from outer space takes on a very different form that is blob-like. This film was actually released to be the second ("B") movie in a double feature, with *I Married a Monster from Outer Space* as the lead title. At the time, these double features were designed to appeal to teenagers, and they were shown primarily at drive-in theatres. *The Blob* seemed more popular, so it was quickly given primary billing. The story line is pretty basic: An alien lifeform comes to Earth and terrorizes a small town in Pennsylvania, consuming all humans in its path. It grows bigger and bloodier (a pulsating red color added a nice touch), and it is found to be indestructible. Somewhat by accident, the movie's hero figures out that cold can stop it, so the military ships the nasty mess off to the Arctic. The story is silly and the acting is pathetic. It was the first role for a 28-year old actor billed as "Steven McQueen." He went on to be a big star and likely denied how he got his start. But *The Blob* has endured; the town of Phoenixville, PA, for example, holds an annual "Blobfest."

Photo credit: Movie poster, The Blob, bigdogLHR, Flickr.com, CC BY 2.0

## The Ten Commandments (Spectacle)

While Boomer kids might have been fond of horror and science fiction, they were astonished by epic spectacles. The 50s and 60s saw a new movement toward more elaborate films with big stories, big musical scores, big casts, big sets, big special effects and big budgets. These movies focused on different subject matter, but many of them were historical in nature. *The Ten Commandments* (1956) by Cecil B. DeMille was not only indicative of an epic spectacle, it was at the time the most expensive movie ever made. It told the Biblical story of Moses, a baby who was found and raised to be an Egyptian prince. He learns of his Jewish roots and ultimately leads the Jews out of Egypt. *The Ten Commandments* was filmed on location in Egypt, featured major stars (Charlton Heston as Moses), a "cast of thousands," and award-winning special effects. The movie made more money than any other film in 1956 and was the second most successful movie of the 50s. Other epic spectacles of the era include *The Robe* (1953), *Ben-Hur* (1959), *Spartacus* (1960), *Exodus* (1960), *El Cid* (1961), *Lawrence of Arabia* (1962) and *Dr. Zhivago* (1965).

Photo credit: Movie poster, The Ten Commandments, 1956, public domain

## Cleopatra (Spectacle)

Not every epic spectacle was a winner. *Cleopatra*, a 1963 movie directed by Joseph L. Mankiewicz and starring Elizabeth Taylor and Richard Burton, eclipsed *The Ten Commandments* in its expense. It was plagued by problems from the beginning, which included changing casts, directors, locales and sets, all of which led to massive cost overruns that nearly sent its studio, 20th Century Fox, into bankruptcy. The adulterous relationship of its co-stars may have been intriguing to moviegoers, but it didn't make producing the movie any easier. Mankiewicz was quoted as claiming *Cleopatra* was "the toughest three pictures I ever made." In fact, the movie was a four-hour train wreck. It had the dubious distinction of being the only film to gross more than any other movie during the year (nearly $58 million in the U.S. and Canada) while still losing money because of its production and marketing costs. It was not a critical success. But Taylor and Burton sure made headlines; they went on to marry twice and watch both their careers decline, making only one more good movie together (*Who's Afraid of Virginia Woolf?*).

Photo credit: Movie poster, Cleopatra, incorporates art by Howard Terpning, 1963, public domain

## James Bond Movies (Spy)

The Cold War was very good for the movie business. In 1953, Ian Fleming first published a story featuring the British spy James Bond aka 007, "Licensed to Kill." Fleming probably never suspected his Bond series would lead to one of the most successful film franchises in history. James Bond movies typify the spy genre: They celebrate a modern-day spy superhero, engaging in global exploits, with a healthy dose of beautiful women and nasty villains. Unlike most comic book figures, however, this hero is not superhuman – he's just exceptionally good at getting out of jams and staying alive. Sean Connery played James Bond to perfection in such classics as *Dr. No* (1962), *From Russia with Love* (1963), *Goldfinger* (1964) and others. Connery was the "Bond" older Boomers knew, but Roger Moore may be more familiar to younger Boomers. A few other actors took on the Bond role, but I personally think Connery and Moore were the best at it. A remarkable twenty-six Bond films have been made, and very likely there are more to come. Lucky Boomers have been able to literally grow up with James Bond.

Photo credit: NO-18-F001, Johan Oomen, Flickr.com, CC BY-SA 2.0

### Come Spy with Me (Spy)

The spy genre was so popular that some film studios began to make B movie versions of them, appealing to adolescents and teens. Most of these, like the 1967 movie, *Come Spy with Me*, had little merit. This unfortunate film from ABC Circle Films starred Troy Donahue, who had just ended his contract with Warner Bros., and Andrea Dromm, who was trying to leverage her success in the 1966 film, *The Russians are Coming, The Russians are Coming*. Dromm played the lead role as an "agent" who manages to thwart an assassination plot, rescue a kidnap victim, solve a murder, and still have time to dance "the Shark" on the island of Jamaica. The only notable part of the movie may have been the title song, performed by Smokey Robinson & the Miracles. It was panned by critics and audiences alike. That same year saw the release of two other female spy films, *Caprice* starring Doris Day, and *Fathom* starring Raquel Welch. Scores of spy films came out in the 60s – not all of them good.

Photo credit: Troy Donahue, kate gabrielle, Flickr.com, CC BY 2.0

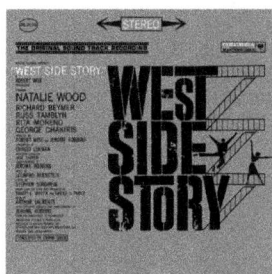

### West Side Story (Youth)

Filmmakers were very aware of America's burgeoning youth culture, driven by the baby boom of the 50s and 60s. They rushed to make movies about youth as well as for youth. In 1957, a Broadway musical called *West Side Story* debuted. In addition to memorable music by Leonard Bernstein, the show retold the love story of Shakespeare's *Romeo and Juliet* in a contemporary New York setting, updating the Montagues and Capulets to street gangs the "Jets" and "Sharks." The show was adapted to film in 1961, making the musical more widely available. Even as a 13-year old, I remember being enthralled by the story, and I love watching it to this day. I wasn't the only ardent fan; *West Side Story*, directed by Robert Wise, won ten Academy Awards, including Best Picture. It also won rave reviews and brought in over $44 million worldwide. A remake of this classic, directed by Steven Spielberg, is scheduled for late 2020. Other winning movies of the era that focused on youth included *Rebel Without a Cause* (1955), *The Graduate* (1967) and *Easy Rider* (1969).

Photo credit: Various artists – West Side Story movie soundtrack, 1961, Lawren, Flickr.com, CC BY 2.0

## Beach Party Movies (Youth)

On the other side of the youth movie spectrum were such forgettable productions as the series of beach party movies (1963 through 1968) from American International Pictures (AIP). These films generally featured light-hearted simplistic storylines, activities of interest to teens, such as drag racing, surfing, smoking, drinking and making out, and bathing-suit clad stars, most notably Frankie Avalon and former Mouseketeer Annette Funicello. AIP is often credited with starting the beach party movie craze; the studio created twelve such films, including *Beach Party* (1963), *Muscle Beach Party* (1964), *Bikini Beach* (1964) and *Beach Blanket Bingo* (1965). Despite their substandard quality, these films were profitable and very popular with teen audiences. Beach party movies were not the first movies to feature frolicking teens. In fact, beach party movies were probably inspired by the films *Gidget* (1959) and *Gidget Goes Hawaiian* (1961). Also, lest we forget, the superstar Elvis Presley made a series of B teen movies from the mid 50s to the late 60s.

Photo credit: Publicity photo of Frankie Avalon and Annette Funicello depicting their roles in the series of Beach Party films they popularized during the mid-60s, public domain

### How the West was Won (Western)

The venerable Western had great success on television in the 50s and 60s, but the big screen also did wonders for this genre. The 1962 blockbuster, *How the West was Won*, is proof of that. This film also qualifies as an epic spectacle because of its large format (one of only two films made using wide-screen "Cinerama"), the way the story was told (five segments, each with different directors and locales), the elaborate musical score and the multi-star cast. Since the movie studio MGM had success with other epic spectacles such as *Ben-Hur*, it was felt an epic Western would work just as well. Still, the highly unusual idea to follow generations of a family through five time periods was not without risk, and the $15 million budget was substantial. *How the West was Won* garnered three Academy Awards and was a huge success. The movie made over $46 million in North America and was the second highest-grossing film of 1963. It also was responsible for influencing a television series of the same name, as well as a comic book adaptation.

Photo credit: Movie poster, How the West was Won, public domain

## Gunfight at Comanche Creek (Western)

As with other popular movie genres, the Western spawned B movie versions in the 1930s and 1940s, as well as the 50s and 60s. These second tier, low budget productions often starred no-name actors. The 1963 movie, *Gunfight at Comanche Creek*, exemplifies the B Western, except that it did feature a bona fide star, Audie Murphy. Murphy was a decorated World War II soldier who was discovered by James Cagney. Murphy's acting career lasted from 1948 to 1969, during which time he made numerous movies, many of them Westerns. *Gunfight a Comanche Creek* was an unremarkable film in which Murphy played a detective who goes undercover to foil a gang of bank robbers. The movie appeared two years after Murphy's 1961 television show, "Whispering Smith," which lasted just twenty episodes. Other B Westerns of the time that starred the war hero: *Ride Clear of Diablo* (1954), *Posse from Hell* (1961), *Apache Rifles* (1964), *Bullet for a Badman* (1964), and *The Quick Gun* (1964).

Photo credit: Photo of Audie Murphy as Tom Smith in television program, "Whispering Smith," 1961, public domain

## Sources

*If you would like free access to a special webpage that includes all of the source links from this book, simply send your email address to: guidewordspub@gmail.com. In the subject line, type: WL Links. Your email will remain private and will not be shared or sold.*

*Movies*
https://livinghistoryfarm.org/farminginthe50s/life_18.html

*Lady and the Tramp (Animation)*
https://en.wikipedia.org/wiki/Lady_and_the_Tramp
https://en.wikipedia.org/wiki/List_of_Walt_Disney_Pictures_films#1960s

*Hey There, It's Yogi Bear! (Animation)*
https://en.wikipedia.org/wiki/Hey_There,_It%27s_Yogi_Bear!
https://www.nytimes.com/1964/07/30/archives/hey-there-its-yogi-bear-new-color-cartoon-opens-here.html

*Creature from the Black Lagoon*
http://www.horrorfilmhistory.com/index.php?pageID=1950sa
https://en.wikipedia.org/wiki/Creature_from_the_Black_Lagoon

*House on Haunted Hill*
https://en.wikipedia.org/wiki/House_on_Haunted_Hill
https://en.wikipedia.org/wiki/William_Castle

*The Day the Earth Stood Still*
https://en.wikipedia.org/wiki/The_Day_the_Earth_Stood_Still

*The Blob*
https://en.wikipedia.org/wiki/The_Blob

*The Ten Commandments*
https://en.wikipedia.org/wiki/The_Ten_Commandments_(1956_film)

*Cleopatra*
https://en.wikipedia.org/wiki/Cleopatra_(1963_film)

https://www.vanityfair.com/news/1998/03/elizabeth-taylor-199803

*James Bond Movies*
https://en.wikipedia.org/wiki/Production_of_the_James_Bond_films#Thunderball_(1965)

*Come Spy with Me*
https://en.wikipedia.org/wiki/Come_Spy_with_Me_(film)

*West Side Story*
https://en.wikipedia.org/wiki/West_Side_Story_(1961_film)

*Beach Party Movies*
https://en.wikipedia.org/wiki/Beach_party_film

*How the West was Won*
https://en.wikipedia.org/wiki/How_the_West_Was_Won_(film)

*Gunfight at Comanche Creek*
https://en.wikipedia.org/wiki/Gunfight_at_Comanche_Creek
https://en.wikipedia.org/wiki/Audie_Murphy

# The Ultimate Boomer Brand Winner & Loser

My goal in writing this book was to take you on an enjoyable, nostalgic journey of the brands Boomer kids grew up with in the 50s and 60s. I tried to spice it up a bit by using an unashamedly subjective point of view to select brands that I considered to be either winners or losers.

Before closing, I want to cast my vote for two brands that stand above, and below, all others: The Ultimate Boomer Brand Winner and The Ultimate Boomer Brand Loser. It may well be an exercise in futility to choose just one brand that rises to the top and just one brand that falls to the depths, but I hope you'll see the wisdom of my choices – even if you might not agree.

## The Ultimate Winner: DISNEY

Very simply, there is no other company, or brand, quite like Disney.

In its 2018 fiscal year, Disney generated over $59 billion in revenue with a market capitalization of $150 billion. Among its media holdings are ABC, ESPN and 100-plus Disney-branded cable networks. Disney acquired Twentieth Century Fox, including both the movie studio and television properties, in 2019. From 2015 through 2018, Disney-produced movies generated more revenue internationally than any other movies. Disney owns theme parks, including Disneyland, Disney World and several international parks. Disney operates a cruise line with ships that dock at its own private island. Almost $5 billion worth of consumer products were sold by Disney in 2018.

You could legitimately claim that the modern-day Disney, founded in 1923 by Walt Disney, truly emerged during the 50s and 60s. The Boomer era is when Disney really hit its stride.

As indicated in the "Movies" chapter, Disney dominated children's films in the 50s and 60s. Its animated movies set such a high bar that they were unequalled. Disney was a powerhouse on television as well, producing the incredibly popular

"Mickey Mouse Club" (1955 – 1958) as well as several Disney prime time shows, beginning with "Walt Disney Presents" in 1958 and culminating in "The Wonderful World of Disney."

Disneyland opened in Anaheim, California in 1955, creating the "theme park" category. In its first ten years of operation, Disneyland welcomed fifty million visitors. Some Boomer kids may have been lucky enough to visit Disneyland during their family travels.

Disney World debuted in Orlando, Florida in 1971, overshadowing Disneyland to become the greatest theme park ever built. Today Disney World is the world's most visited vacation resort, attracting over 52 million visitors each year. Disney pioneered crowd control at its parks and is a recognized global innovator in customer service.

Boomer kids grew up immersed in Disney cartoons, movies, television shows, records and books. Kids fell in love with their favorite Disney characters, whether it was Cinderella, Peter Pan, Mickey Mouse, Donald Duck or Pluto. Chances are one or more of these characters appeared on kids' clothing, on their lunch boxes and in their toy boxes – maybe even on the wallpaper in their rooms. And every kid I knew wore "Mouseketeer ears" or a "Davy Crockett" hat.

If any company really nails it when it comes to giving kids what they dream of, it was, and still is, Disney. That's why Disney is the ultimate Boomer Brand Winner.

Photo credit: Mickey Mouse, Disney parade, MacGyverNRW on Pixabay.com

## The Ultimate Loser: HOWARD JOHNSON'S

Remember Howard Johnson's, the roadside chain of orange and blue restaurants that families loved to stop at in the 50s and 60s? New Englander Howard Johnson first had the idea to franchise restaurants, preparing food in a central location and shipping it to franchisees so he could control the quality. Kids craved "HoJo" hot dogs (called "frankforts"), split down the middle and grilled in butter, nestled in a toasted white bread bun. HoJo's is where I got my first introduction to belly-less fried clam strips, and I loved them. But Howard Johnson's "28 flavors" of ice cream, which no one else could match, was the absolute best thing about the restaurant.

There were over 1,000 locations, all of them consistently serving up good food by well-trained, well-dressed friendly waitstaff. The restaurants were mostly on turnpikes and other major roads, fronted by large neon signs with the Howard Johnson's name and its kid-friendly logo: Simple Simon and the Pieman. By 1965, the chain's revenues exceeded Burger King, McDonald's and Kentucky Fried Chicken *combined*. That's right, Howard Johnson's was the undisputed restaurant chain champion. More than 500 Howard Johnson Motor Lodges were added to the brand portfolio, as well as a line of frozen foods.

What happened? How did such an iconic, beloved brand virtually disappear? It turns out that those "motor lodges" were a last-ditch effort to save the Howard Johnson's moniker. By the 1970s, the restaurant business had dramatically changed, thanks to the "QSR" (Quick Service Restaurant) phenomenon I wrote about in the "Fast Food" chapter. Howard Johnson's restaurants looked old-fashioned and the menu was out of step with evolving tastes. Cheap burgers, chicken and pizza served fast ruled the day. Too many aggressive competitors saturated the marketplace and stole the limelight. The Howard Johnson's approach seemed antiquated. A few HoJos hung on, mostly for nostalgic reasons, to no avail.

While Howard Johnson's is my choice for the ultimate Boomer Brand Loser, its name still has some appeal, especially for nostalgic adult Boomers. While you're not likely to see any new restaurants adorned with the name, Wyndham Hotels has purchased the rights to the brand. Wyndham is in the process of opening new Howard Johnson hotels, complete with retro décor. The brand lives on, even if it is in a different life form.

Photo credit: Entrance to a Howard Johnson's restaurant, PA, photograph by Christopher Ziemnowicz, public domain

## Sources

*If you would like free access to a special webpage that includes all of the source links from this book, simply send your email address to: guidewordspub@gmail.com. In the subject line, type: WL Links. Your email will remain private and will not be shared or sold.*

*Disney*
https://www.msn.com/en-us/money/companies/the-colossal-disney-conglomerate-in-numbers/ss-BBTLC1q#image=1
https://magicguides.com/disney-world-statistics/

*Howard Johnson's*
http://www.hojoland.com/
https://www.kiplinger.com/article/business/T062-C000-S001-whatever-happened-to-howard-johnson-s-restaurants.html

The following trademarks and registered trademarks are the property of their respective holders: ABC, Burger King, Disney, Disneyland, Disney World, Donald Duck, ESPN, HoJo, Howard Johnson, Kentucky Fried Chicken, McDonald's, Mickey Mouse, Mouseketeer, Pluto, The Wonderful World of Disney, Twentieth Century Fox, Walt Disney Presents, Wyndham Hotels, 28 flavors

# Goodies for Boomer Brand Enthusiasts

Here's what you'll find in this Appendix section:

**Pick Your Boomer Brand Winners and Losers**

Which Boomer Brands do *you* consider the best and the worst? Use this handy fill-in form to make your own choices.

**Watch Vintage Commercials... and More**

Links to TV commercials for the brands covered in this book.

**The Brands in *BOOMER BRANDS***

A list of the brands that appear in my first book on the topic.

**Boomer Brands Discussion Guide**

How to stimulate conversation around "Boomer Brands."

# Pick Your Boomer Brand Winners and Losers

Fill in the Boomer Brands you think are the best and worst in each category. There are no right or wrong answers – your opinion is all that matters!

## Television
Winners

_____

_____

_____

_____

Losers

_____

_____

_____

_____

## Cereal
Winners

_____

_____

_____

_____

Losers

_____

_____

_____

_____

## Soft Drinks

Winners

_____

_____

_____

_____

Losers

_____

_____

_____

_____

## Snack Foods

Winners

_____

_____

_____

_____

Losers

_____

_____

_____

_____

## Convenience Foods

Winners

_____

_____

_____

_____

Losers

_____

_____

_____

_____

## Toys, Games and Comic Books

Winners

_____

_____

_____

_____

Losers

_____

_____

_____

_____

## Health, Beauty and Cigarettes
Winners

_____

_____

_____

_____

Losers

_____

_____

_____

_____

## Automobiles
Winners

_____

_____

_____

Losers

_____

_____

_____

_____

## Fast Food

Winners

_____

_____

_____

_____

Losers

_____

_____

_____

_____

## Rock 'n' Roll

Winners

_____

_____

_____

_____

Losers

_____

_____

_____

_____

## Revolution

Winners

_____

_____

_____

_____

Losers

_____

_____

_____

_____

## Environment

Winners

_____

_____

_____

_____

Losers

_____

_____

_____

_____

## Technology
Winners

_____

_____

_____

_____

Losers

_____

_____

_____

_____

## Movies
Winners

_____

_____

_____

_____

Losers

_____

_____

_____

_____

**Your Choice for the Ultimate Boomer Brand Winner:**

_____

**Your Choice for the Ultimate Boomer Brand Loser:**

_____

# Watch Vintage TV Commercials... and More

The following URL links coordinate with the brands covered in this book. These links will also be included on the "Sources" webpage (see Introduction for how to access the webpage). *Please note:* All of these links are to YouTube.com and they are subject to change without notice. Linking to these videos does not imply endorsement. The publisher is not responsible for the content of the videos.

(W=Winner, L=Loser)

## Television

*(television episodes)*

W The Adventures of Superman
https://youtu.be/wA1SPhGhvHU
L Pinky Lee Show
https://youtu.be/Xri0zbSzuds
W The Adventures of Rin Tin Tin
https://youtu.be/Hixyso78qaw
L Captain Gallant of the Foreign Legion
https://youtu.be/JsgpNrP0M5I
W The Adventures of Ozzie and Harriet
https://youtu.be/u4efyzwsT6s
L My Favorite Martian
https://youtu.be/lf5Chh88dXE
W Sea Hunt
https://youtu.be/BqCIEr8AFgs
L Circus Boy
https://youtu.be/UG2ziXY7sd0
W Lassie
https://youtu.be/HluWrXiVNks
L Mr. Ed
https://youtu.be/a_T-EeC1xJk
W The Flintstones
https://youtu.be/bybsr1ysczY
L The Jetsons
https://youtu.be/1oDaHRbIDH8
W Bonanza
https://youtu.be/yJAQ-HdG9K0

L The Big Valley
https://youtu.be/anthFFqWLfc
W Candid Camera
https://youtu.be/PU40VQsgZog
L Twenty-One
https://youtu.be/CVnGLks--oA
W The Ed Sullivan Show
https://youtu.be/jenWdylTtzs
L The Sonny and Cher Comedy Hour
https://youtu.be/WXKuMwKLL20
W Jonny Quest
https://youtu.be/U79al1GPvmg
L The Dudley Do-Right Show
https://youtu.be/dtvsGgPfMYk

**Cereal**
*(commercials)*
W Cap'n Crunch
https://youtu.be/uZSjFtdKcCU
L Quake
https://youtu.be/Q-sTnm_aPBY
W Cocoa Puffs and Cocoa Krispies
https://youtu.be/7uVP1Uy5tL0
L Sugar Jets
https://youtu.be/cyKl_saKtP4
W Froot Loops
https://youtu.be/GSp3eHDYAx8
L Kellogg's OKs
https://youtu.be/kcTMqN7_Fp0
W Lucky Charms
https://youtu.be/-haC7h4dAR0
L Nabisco Rice Honeys
https://youtu.be/05SiLbCJKkI
W Trix
https://youtu.be/35M0vtwgy9g
L Maypo
https://youtu.be/sz7IdA11n3U

## Soft Drinks

(commercials)

W Dr Pepper
https://youtu.be/l1gZkf_-UyI
L Royal Crown Cola
https://youtu.be/RT8fhKun6p8
W 7UP
https://youtu.be/morho_sUqs4
L Squirt
https://youtu.be/B_cbSiUdnaU
W Sprite
https://youtu.be/3WgIxbSMTHY
L Nesbitt's
https://youtu.be/mlo_Kdscw_A
W TaB
https://youtu.be/qXu3zTqlY_Q
L Flav-R-Straws
https://youtu.be/FGAIJ37nyrM
W Kool-Aid
https://youtu.be/yKY2O4KFmMU
L Funny Face
https://youtu.be/Bn-tpSSnSrs

## Snack Foods

*(commercials)*

W Barnum's Animal Crackers
https://youtu.be/1JF5hsUnz5Q
L Atomic Fireballs
None
W Cheetos
https://youtu.be/Na6t213G-V0
L E-Z Pop
https://youtu.be/YjQnM68IORg
W Drake's
https://youtu.be/toOMzNXwiQk
L Bonomo Turkish Taffy

https://youtu.be/Jpw64PkCJn8
W M & Ms
https://youtu.be/yn_096mMGc0
L Necco Wafers
None
W Popsicle
https://youtu.be/LctFS4kLG3I
L Pixy Stix
None

## Convenience Foods
(commercials)
W PB&J
https://youtu.be/BumyAqVoJL0
L Smucker's Goober
None
W Catsup/Ketchup
https://youtu.be/vbmfNltw_U4
L SPAM
https://youtu.be/gLRPJE0QBQQ
W Log Cabin Syrup
https://youtu.be/-fJIIorEu1I
L Aunt Jemima
https://youtu.be/beOxrAt2L4w
W Kraft Singles
https://youtu.be/s_aPDRz4lHk
L SpaghettiOs
https://youtu.be/Kq_L1uP7AUQ
W Pop-Tarts
https://youtu.be/Fj6uP5r-ID0
L Space Food Sticks
https://youtu.be/KPZ8HHRR1A0

## Toys, Games and Comic Books
(commercials)
W Barbie
https://youtu.be/9hhjjhYGQtY

L Cap Gun
https://youtu.be/xi0op4Fsbd8
W Comic Books
https://youtu.be/dYFwQoh7nG0
L ERECTOR Set
https://youtu.be/Sg4nLViwEmg
W Paint by Numbers
None
L Sea-Monkeys
https://youtu.be/Y-tInARFVNs
W Easy-Bake Oven
https://youtu.be/XcYoghee5Sc
L Twister
https://youtu.be/8g2eEZu_0L4
W Mr. Potato Head
https://youtu.be/ICGrjmJouWA
L Slinky
https://youtu.be/RB9a3OkHvmA

**Health, Beauty and Cigarettes**
(*commercials*)
W Clairol
https://youtu.be/Be9MREGx7NM
L Brylcreem
https://youtu.be/o6F4GtyRfto
W Dove
https://youtu.be/jWDoco3qFpI
L Chux
None
W Crest
https://youtu.be/92lBPkfefmo
L Ipana
https://youtu.be/bT3snZo5StQ
W Secret
https://youtu.be/-EEETMUr8gU
L Buster Brown Shoes
https://youtu.be/Pm4xH9unqzU

W Marlboro
https://youtu.be/wibHcZ4FNbU
L Camel
https://youtu.be/gCMzjJjuxQI

**Automobiles**
*(commercials)*
W 1957 Chevrolet
https://youtu.be/GU-SRHV-2uk
L 1959 Cadillac
https://youtu.be/bX_sstIKMBQ
W Ford Thunderbird
https://youtu.be/5UqWTvpzp1Y
L Ford Edsel
https://youtu.be/-ysGpk9ONxw
W Pontiac GTO
https://youtu.be/YXF4YVFpHFw
L Crosley Hotshot
None
W Shelby Cobra
https://youtu.be/t9MjY-mpspI
L Amphicar
https://youtu.be/LObRwKsKUxw
W VW Beetle
https://youtu.be/tc-kekzH2dU
L Studebaker Lark
https://youtu.be/6fd_Fw2c0pQ

**Fast Food**
*(commercials)*
W Burger King
https://youtu.be/NSvnw3tvPSk
L Burger Chef
https://youtu.be/OvYrG5ny6vM
W Chick-fil-A
https://youtu.be/ElexlOm5H98
L Horn & Hardart

None
W Dunkin' Donuts
https://youtu.be/petqFm94osQ
L LUM'S
https://youtu.be/zI2bV2UBqrY
W SONIC
https://youtu.be/c90YbjO-uGo
L BONANZA and PONDEROSA
https://youtu.be/DDQM0BFXWG4
W SUBWAY
https://youtu.be/_wkiHZkDFu4
L Blimpie
https://youtu.be/e7-ySEsjW-s

**Rock 'n' Roll**
*(TV performances, some commercials)*
W "American Pie"
https://youtu.be/iX_TFkut1PM
L Eve of Destruction
https://youtu.be/ntLsElbW9X0
W The Beach Boys
https://youtu.be/2s4slliAtQU
L Jan & Dean
https://youtu.be/c2GwDGjiV4k
W The British Invasion
https://youtu.be/Qyclqo_AV2M
L Novelty Songs
https://youtu.be/9Gc4QTqslN4
W The Byrds
https://youtu.be/umwkVoZgdqk
L "Louie Louie" by The Kingsmen
https://youtu.be/CCYobAPLZ1w
W Soul Train
https://youtu.be/qXbP4JBf8T0
L Shindig!
https://youtu.be/-LsFJYr95Ac

## Revolution

*(TV coverage)*

W Jesse Jackson

https://youtu.be/HHd6XYMlP4I

L George Wallace

None

W Robert F. Kennedy

https://youtu.be/jkbW5yJanzc

L 1968 Democratic National Convention

https://youtu.be/aUKzSsVmnpY

W Peace Sign

None

L Vietnam War

https://youtu.be/g_2d3sDITYs

W Whole Earth Catalog

None

L LSD

None

W Ms. magazine

None

L Watergate

https://youtu.be/OZSGMMUC7FQ

## Environment

*(commercials, TV coverage)*

W The Nature Conservancy

https://youtu.be/OMYcc3Zn5a8

L Big Oil

https://youtu.be/OSZgk9iSykk

W Environmental Defense Fund

https://youtu.be/YuPwS3mD3kk

L Smog

None

W Earth Day

https://youtu.be/5v_2nTvAcSU

L Coal

None

W Greenpeace
https://youtu.be/pxwtPCX8-EA
L Three Mile Island
https://youtu.be/eGI7VymjSho
W Patagonia
https://youtu.be/3VmjDNLo-lE
L Plastics
https://youtu.be/hiXGiCaBxtM

## Technology
*(commercials)*
W 45 rpm Record
None
L 8-Track Tape
None
W Transistor Radio
None
L de Havilland DH 106 Comet Jetliner
None
W Polaroid Land Camera
https://youtu.be/b2Te3HowZuE
L Kodak Instamatic Camera
https://youtu.be/GB3YqMPCpUM
W Xerox 924 Copier
https://youtu.be/swyqrf1PZjg
L View-Master
https://youtu.be/DAxJzwawc7g
W Touch-Tone Telephone
None
L First U.S. Satellite Launch
None

## Movies
*(movie trailers)*
W Lady and the Tramp (Animation)
https://youtu.be/LZmVm6qv1Lk
L Hey There, It's Yogi Bear! (Animation)

https://youtu.be/ghhAeQAaedA
W Creature from the Black Lagoon (Horror)
https://youtu.be/svyPswixryM
L House on Haunted Hill (Horror)
https://youtu.be/Bsa9ymSDoJo
W The Day the Earth Stood Still (Science Fiction)
https://youtu.be/OfpSXI8_UpY
L The Blob (Science Fiction)
https://youtu.be/TdUsyXQ8Wrs
W The Ten Commandments (Spectacle)
https://youtu.be/1LKUpWvnubU
L Cleopatra (Spectacle)
https://youtu.be/SCzCLgNcDjM
W James Bond Movies (Spy)
https://youtu.be/pw61uyAoF8A
L Come Spy with Me (Spy)
None
W West Side Story (Youth)
https://youtu.be/IakuITGwcoU
L Beach Party Movies (Youth)
https://youtu.be/nkhGmZPJIHY
W How the West was Won (Western)
https://youtu.be/gW9o2nR11DM
L Gunfight at Comanche Creek (Western)
None

**The Ultimate Boomer Brand Winner and Loser**
*(commercials)*
W Disney
https://youtu.be/hLwBVdUggLs
L Howard Johnson's
https://youtu.be/pgmbQ6tN_Ko

# The Brands in *BOOMER BRANDS*

If you enjoyed reading this book, you might also like the first book on the topic, *BOOMER BRANDS: Iconic Brands that Shaped Our Childhood*. Here is a list of the "Boomer Brand Cameos" that appear in *BOOMER BRANDS*.

## View Tube (Television)
Bozo the Clown
Huckleberry Hound
Mr. Wizard
Westerns

## Bowled Over (Cereal)
Kellogg's Frosted Flakes
Cheerios
Alpha-Bits
Life

## Soda Pop-ular (Soft Drinks)
The Cola Wars
Fruit Juice Frenzy
Tang

## Snack Attack (Snack Foods)
Bubble Gum
Good Humor
Oreo
Twinkies

## Faster Foods (Convenience Foods)
Cheese Whiz
Jell-O

Ovaltine

## Playtime (Toys, Games and Comic Books)
Board Games
LEGO
MAD
WIFFLE Ball

## The Dazzle of Disney (Disney)
Mickey Mouse Ears
Disney Parks and Resorts
Disney Merchandising

## Lookin' Good, Feelin' Good (Health, Beauty and Cigarettes)
Clearasil
Coppertone
The Pill
Virginia Slims

## On the Road Again (Automobiles)
Corvette
Mustang
Texaco

## Orange You Hungry? (Howard Johnson's)
HoJo Brands

## Burgers Galore and More (Fast Food)
Kentucky Fried Chicken
McDonald's
Pizza Hut

**Reelin' and Rockin' (Rock 'n' Roll)**
American Bandstand
The Monkees
Motown

**Politics and Protest (Revolution)**
Black Panther Party
Eugene McCarthy
Woodstock

**Green Scene (Environment)**
Keep America Beautiful
Tom's of Maine
Whole Foods

**Ten Boomer Era Brands with Lasting Legacies**
Alka-Seltzer
Credit Card
Gatorade
Holiday Inn
Hush Puppies
Microwave Oven
Radio Shack
Target
Timex
Trader Joe's

**Also included:**
The Boomer Era, Year by Year
(1946 – 1964)

# Boomer Brands Discussion Guide

The goal of this book and my first book, *BOOMER BRANDS*, is to take Boomers on a nostalgic journey. The brands Boomers were introduced to as kids bring back childhood memories. One reason we recollect brands, TV shows, songs and events from long ago is that we associate them with the comfort and security of our childhood homes. Brands from the past can act as an emotional trigger, setting off positive feelings and shielding us from today's pressing problems. Research into sharing nostalgic memories indicates it is good for the psyche and actually counteracts loneliness.

You can use brands from your childhood to stimulate conversation between yourself and a friend, sibling, spouse or parent. You can also use brands to engage in spirited conversation with a group of friends, relatives, or co-workers who are Boomers. It would even be fun to organize an inter-generational brand discussion group.

To spark conversation, here are some questions to consider. Use the categories and brands in this book to guide your answers.

- Which childhood brands did you like the most? The least?
- Is there a childhood TV show, movie, product, song or event that significantly influenced your life? Which one, and why?
- Pick a brand you liked as a kid that still exists today. How has that brand remained the same and how has it changed over time? How do you feel about the brand today vs. as a kid?
- Some childhood brands that disappeared are making a comeback to appeal to Boomer adults. Think of a brand that has done this. Do you like the retro brand? Why or why not?

- Choose a childhood brand that appealed to you as a kid and a modern-day brand from the same category. The modern-day brand should be one that wasn't around when you were a kid but, ideally, it should appeal to today's kids. (This would be a great exercise for an inter-generational discussion.)

Compare and contrast one brand with the other as follows:

  o How do the names compare?

  o How do the graphics and packaging compare?

  o What attributes did your childhood brand have that made it appealing to you as a kid? What attributes does the modern-day brand have that makes it appealing to kids? What are the differences and similarities?

  o How was your childhood brand promoted to kids as compared to the modern-day brand? Consider media used, creative approaches used, and calls to action.

  o Did your childhood brand sponsor a children's television program, or was it advertised on a children's television program? Does the modern-day brand use any kind of tie-in with media directed to children?

  o How effectively do you think your childhood brand was marketed given the period? How effectively is the modern-day brand being marketed?

I hope these questions inspire you to have lively and engaging conversations about Boomer Brands!

# Index

In order to make this index more useful, it is set up in a non-conventional way. References to "Winners" and "Losers" are indexed alphabetically within each chapter rather than as part of a consolidated index.

**Introduction: Still Relevant After All These Years** ........... 7 – 11

**Television** ...................................................................... 13 – 37

Adventures of Superman .................................... 15

The Pinky Lee Show ............................................ 16

Adventures of Rin Tin Tin ................................. 17

Captain Gallant of the Foreign Legion .......... 18

The Adventures of Ozzie and Harriet ........... 19

My Favorite Martian ......................................... 20

Sea Hunt .............................................................. 21

Circus Boy ........................................................... 22

Lassie .................................................................... 23

Mr. Ed .................................................................. 24

The Flintstones ................................................... 25

The Jetsons .......................................................... 26

Bonanza ............................................................... 27

The Big Valley ..................................................... 28

Candid Camera ................................................... 29

Twenty-One ......................................................... 30

The Ed Sullivan Show ....................................... 31

The Sonny and Cher Comedy Hour .............. 32

Jonny Quest ......................................................... 33

The Dudley Do-Right Show ............................. 34

Sources ............................................. 35

## Cereal ......................................................... 39 – 52

Cap'n Crunch ...................................... 41

Quake .................................................... 42

Cocoa Puffs and Cocoa Krispies .................... 43

Sugar Jets ............................................. 44

Froot Loops ........................................... 45

Kellogg's OKs ......................................... 46

Lucky Charms ......................................... 47

Nabisco Rice Honeys .............................. 48

Trix ....................................................... 49

Maypo ................................................... 50

Sources ................................................. 51

## Soft Drinks ................................................... 53 – 66

Dr Pepper .............................................. 55

Royal Crown Cola ................................... 56

7UP ....................................................... 57

Squirt .................................................... 58

Sprite .................................................... 59

Nesbitt's ................................................ 60

TaB ....................................................... 61

Flav-R-Straws ........................................ 62

Kool-Aid ............................................... 63

Funny Face ............................................ 64

Sources ................................................. 65

**Snack Foods** ............................................................. 67 – 80

Barnum's Animal Crackers ............................ 69

Atomic Fireballs ................................................ 70

Cheetos ............................................................... 71

E-Z Pop ............................................................... 72

Drake's ................................................................. 73

Bonomo Turkish Taffy ...................................... 74

M & M's ............................................................... 75

Necco Wafers ..................................................... 76

Popsicle ............................................................... 77

Pixy Stix .............................................................. 78

Sources ................................................................ 79

**Convenience Foods** ................................................ 81 – 94

PB&J ..................................................................... 83

Smucker's Goober ............................................. 84

Catsup/Ketchup ................................................ 85

SPAM .................................................................... 86

Log Cabin Syrup ............................................... 87

Aunt Jemima ...................................................... 88

Kraft Singles ...................................................... 89

SpaghettiOs ....................................................... 90

Pop-Tarts ............................................................ 91

Space Food Sticks ............................................ 92

Sources ................................................................ 93

**Toys, Games and Comic Books** ........................... 95 – 108

Barbie ................................................................... 97

Cap Gun ....................................................... 98

Comic Books ................................................. 99

ERECTOR Set ................................................ 100

Paint by Numbers .......................................... 101

Sea-Monkeys ................................................ 102

Easy-Bake Oven ............................................ 103

Twister ........................................................ 104

Mr. Potato Head ............................................ 105

Slinky ......................................................... 106

Sources ....................................................... 107

## Health, Beauty and Cigarettes ..................................... 109 – 122

Clairol ........................................................ 111

Brylcreem .................................................... 112

Dove ........................................................... 113

Chux ........................................................... 114

Crest ........................................................... 115

Ipana .......................................................... 116

Secret ......................................................... 117

Buster Brown Shoes ....................................... 118

Marlboro ...................................................... 119

Camel .......................................................... 120

Sources ....................................................... 121

## Automobiles ............................................................ 123 – 136

1957 Chevrolet .............................................. 125

1959 Cadillac ................................................ 126

Ford Thunderbird .......................................... 127

Ford Edsel ....................................... 128

Pontiac GTO ..................................... 129

Crosley Hotshot ................................. 130

Shelby Cobra .................................... 131

Amphicar ........................................ 132

VW Beetle ....................................... 133

Studebaker Lark ................................. 134

Sources ......................................... 135

## Fast Food ............................................ 137 – 150

Burger King ..................................... 139

Burger Chef ..................................... 140

Chick-fil-A ..................................... 141

Horn & Hardart .................................. 142

Dunkin' Donuts .................................. 143

LUM'S ........................................... 144

SONIC ........................................... 145

BONANZA and PONDEROSA ........................... 146

SUBWAY .......................................... 147

Blimpie ......................................... 148

Sources ......................................... 149

## Rock 'n' Roll ......................................... 151– 164

"American Pie" .................................. 153

"Eve of Destruction" ........................... 154

The Beach Boys .................................. 155

Jan & Dean ...................................... 156

The British Invasion ........................... 157

Novelty Songs ........................................ 158

The Byrds ............................................159

"Louie Louie" by The Kingsmen ...................... 160

Soul Train ............................................. 161

Shindig! ................................................ 162

Sources ................................................163

## Revolution ................................................ 165 – 178

Jesse Jackson .......................................... 167

George Wallace ......................................168

Robert F. Kennedy ................................... 169

1968 Democratic National Convention .........170

Peace Sign ............................................ 171

Vietnam War ........................................ 172

Whole Earth Catalog ...............................173

LSD ................................................... 174

Ms. magazine ....................................... 175

Watergate ............................................ 176

Sources ............................................... 177

## Environment ................................................ 179 – 192

The Nature Conservancy ................................ 181

Big Oil ................................................ 182

Environmental Defense Fund ........................ 183

Smog ................................................184

Earth Day ............................................185

Coal ................................................... 186

Greenpeace ........................................... 187

Three Mile Island ..................................188

Patagonia ...........................................189

Plastics ............................................. 190

Sources ............................................. 191

## Technology ................................................ 193 – 206

45 rpm Record .................................... 195

8-Track Tape ...................................... 196

Transistor Radio ................................. 197

de Havilland DH 106 Comet Jetliner ............. 198

Polaroid Land Camera ...........................199

Kodak Instamatic Camera ..................... 200

Xerox 914 Copier ................................ 201

View-Master ...................................... 202

Touch-Tone Telephone ......................... 203

First U.S. Satellite Launch .................... 204

Sources ............................................. 205

## Movies ..................................................... 207 – 224

Lady and the Tramp (Animation) ................. 209

Hey There, It's Yogi Bear! (Animation) ..........210

Creature from the Black Lagoon (Horror) .... 211

House on Haunted Hill (Horror) .................. 212

The Day the Earth Stood Still (Sci Fi) ...........213

The Blob (Sci Fi) ................................. 214

The Ten Commandments (Spectacle) ........... 215

Cleopatra (Spectacle) .......................... 216

James Bond Movies (Spy) ..................... 217

Come Spy with Me (Spy) .................................... 218

West Side Story (Youth) .................................... 219

Beach Party Movies (Youth) ............................ 220

How the West was Won (Western) ............... 221

Gunfight at Comanche Creek (Western) ...... 222

Sources ................................................................ 223

## The Ultimate Boomer Brand Winner & Loser ............ 225 – 231

The Ultimate Winner: Disney ......................... 227

The Ultimate Loser: Howard Johnson's ......... 229

Sources ................................................................ 231


Appendix ............................................................ 233

# About the Author

Barry Silverstein is a Boomer, brand historian, freelance writer and retired direct marketing/brand marketing professional. He is the author of numerous non-fiction marketing and small business books, including *BOOMER BRANDS* and *The Breakaway Brand*. He writes "Happily Rewired," (https://happilyrewired.com) a blog for Boomers. Silverstein resides with his wife in the Asheville, North Carolina area. Visit his website:

https://www.barrysilverstein.com

# About the Publisher

GuideWords Publishing publishes books for the Boomer audience. In addition to *Boomer Brand Winners & Losers*, the company published *BOOMER BRANDS*, the first book on this topic. The GuideWords book, *Let's Make Money, Honey: The Couple's Guide to Starting a Service Business*, is designed to help couples succeed in starting and running a small service business.

To learn more about our books, visit our website:

https://www.guidewordspub.com

## Join the conversation about Boomer Brands!

Which childhood brands do you fondly remember? Which childhood brands do you laugh about to this day? Which ones influenced your life? Share your thoughts about "Boomer Brands" on Facebook: https://facebook.com/guidewordspub/

## Did you enjoy reading this book?

Word of mouth is so important to a book's ability to reach the right audience. If you enjoyed reading *Boomer Brand Winners & Losers*, I hope you will consider recommending it to family, friends, and any Boomers you know. A positive online review would also be very much appreciated. And if you haven't read *BOOMER BRANDS*, the first book on the topic, please check it out.

Thank you!
*Barry Silverstein*
https://www.barrysilverstein.com